SUFFERING IS THE ONLY HONEST WORK

A MEMOIR OF LOVE, LOSS, AND DISCOVERY

CASEY AND JIMMY GAUNTT

CONTENTS

INTRODUCTION

Synchronicity–A meaningful coincidence of outer and inner events that are not themselves causally connected. The emphasis lies on meaningful.

Carl Jung

LIFE MAY SEEM like a straight road from birth to death. This event, then the next, the next, and more and more until there are none left. I've experienced great joy and great grief on this road, and all I know for sure is that time weaves through everything, every happening, connecting lives—and deaths—in ways no one can predict, doubling back on itself, stretching itself thin, then snapping back to encompass the past with the future, future with the present. As observed by my favorite poet, Jimmy Gauntt, "This death not even a trailhead on the endless loop through ourselves."

Time is a wanderer, true only to itself. "A little more time," we plead. "Another chance," we beg. But when we stop regretting and start paying attention, the Universe opens the most unexpected gifts.

A MOMENT IN PARIS

MY WIFE, HILARY, and I arrived in Paris on Wednesday, May 13, 2009. Our friends Bill and Terri Stampley had persuaded us to get away for a while from our home in Solana Beach, California, a brief distraction from our relentless grief. The four of us checked into the Hotel d'Aubusson on the left bank of the Seine, where my sister, Laura, seven years my junior, was already settled into a room next to ours. Her husband, Anton, and her two children had stayed behind in their home in Switzerland. After unpacking, we all went out to stroll along leafy boulevards warmed by sun and spring, looking for an outdoor café where we could have lunch and unwind from the flight.

"How about Les Deux Magots?" Laura suggested. "I've been there before and it's great."

"Sure," Hilary said. I knew she was thinking of a lithograph by Michel Delacroix that has hung in our living room for over twenty years, showing that same historic restaurant where Hemingway, Faulkner, and the other literati hung out, and Saint Germain-des-Pres, the oldest cathedral in Paris, that stands directly across the narrow boulevard.

This wasn't our first trip to Paris. In 1995 we had visited the cathedral with our children, Brittany and Jimmy, then fifteen and eleven. Now Les Deux Magots seemed like a meaningful start to this trip.

When we arrived at the restaurant, café-sized tables meant for two or three patrons crowded under the green awning, and waiters scurried around taking orders and delivering meals. I craned my neck, looking for an open spot, but The Two Treasures was absolutely packed.

I turned to our party of five. "We'll need two tables and there's not even one open. We'd better look for a less crowded restaurant." Their faces fell. We had all looked forward to eating here.

And then, amazingly, right in the center of the outdoor patio, directly facing the church, diners at two adjacent tables paid their bills and stood to leave. Perfect!

We wove through the crowd, feeling exceptionally lucky, and settled in. Hilary and Laura sat on my right while I chatted with Terri and Bill on my left. After ordering wine, we surveyed the bustling square before us. People thronged the sidewalk as they do in any city, shoulder to shoulder, weaving in and out on their way to appointments, dates, and business.

Then came a moment that defies explanation.

Laura exclaimed to Hilary, "Oh my God! Did you see *that*?"

I spun around. Tears streamed down the women's cheeks. They stared into the crowd, their faces pale, eyes wide.

I took Hilary's hand, silently asking what was wrong.

She stammered, "I can't talk about it right now! I'll tell you later."

I dropped the subject. She'd tell me what had upset her in her own time. For months her emotions had been roiling as she tried to deal with our tragic loss, and I had learned to respect her sometimes-erratic reactions. We each had another glass of wine and finished our meals. During the walk back to the hotel, Hilary seemed distracted but once more in control.

Once in our room again, she said, "Sit down. I have something unbelievable to tell you."

I did as she asked, wondering what could have left her so shaken.

She twisted her fingers and gazed into my eyes, as if begging me to believe. "As I was watching the crowd I saw a young man dressed in a dark suit carrying a briefcase walk by. His head was down but I could see his intent expression. His cheeks were unnaturally red, and I think that is what drew my attention to him. It wasn't just his face—it was the body, the posture, the gait. When you love someone all his life, he is unmistakable to you. Even when it's actually impossible for him to be there."

I *did* believe her. I focused on her stricken face as she went on.

"In a matter of ten or fifteen seconds he had disappeared into the crowd. I stopped breathing and burst into tears. The next thing I felt was Laura squeezing my thigh and saying, 'Did you see that?'

"I was so grateful to have confirmation that I wasn't hallucinating. Casey, we both saw Jimmy walk past us. It happened so fast I didn't have time to get your attention."

Jimmy! Tears filled my eyes. It just wasn't possible for my sister and Hilary to see Jimmy walk past the Café Les Deux Magots—was it? Yet "impossible" is no longer in our vocabulary.

INTO THE DARKNESS

Nine Months Earlier

SATURDAY MORNING, AUGUST 9th, 2008, dawned bright and clear. Hilary, our daughter, Brittany, and I were busy getting ready to meet my sister and her family for a morning hike. They had flown in from Switzerland and we all were looking forward to some quality family time. Brittany's husband of almost one year, Ryan, was in Alaska fishing with his dad and brothers and she was staying with us.

As I passed Jimmy's room, I glanced in. His battered North Face backpack lay on the chair where he had dumped it the night before, bulging with books and whatever else a twenty-four-year-old needed for a weekend at home. Which probably wasn't much, since his room was exactly as he'd left it when he first went away to college. And he might enjoy a few days away from his "house" in Laurel Canyon, just a couple of miles from Sunset Boulevard in Los Angeles. His place was a cool kind of hippie loft and Jimmy loved it. I begged to differ.

The five-hundred-square-foot cabin on Lookout Mountain Road perched on a cliff behind the landlord's house. A switchback concrete path in poor repair led up to it. The place sported one room that served as a living room, kitchen, and dining area, interrupted by a wooden ladder leading to a sleeping loft too low to stand up in. At some point a tiny room had been added. Jimmy used this as a closet, a home for his stereo system, and a library for his vast collection of books.

A tilting deck with crappy plastic chairs for seating overlooked the canyon. Oak and sycamore provided shade and privacy and looked like they might harbor elves and other fairy-tale creatures. The crudely built hut's one claim to fame was that an out-of-work actor who worked as a carpenter had added on the sleeping loft in lieu of rent. As Jimmy had said, it's a good thing that Harrison Ford made it as an actor because he sure wasn't much of a carpenter.

It was perfect for Jimmy. Only minutes away from Sunset Drive, he could be private, yet close to the entertainment world he was breaking into—the agents, actors, writers that he was getting to know as he worked on his screenplays and acting.

Although not a mansion by any standards, our two-story place in Solana Beach was a comfortable contrast. It had been designed so that the living areas and master bedroom were on the second story to take advantage of the ocean view. The ground floor held the guest room, a smaller living room that we seldom used, and Jimmy's old room, which also served as Hilary's office.

Jimmy and half a dozen friends were flying out next Wednesday for a two-week sea kayaking trip in Vietnam. Other than his shots, the last of which he got Friday just before driving down to our house, and in typical Jimmy fashion, he had made no effort to pack, organize, or even figure out what he needed to take. We had made plans to visit REI later today to outfit him.

With hindsight, both Jimmy and his mother had powerful premonitions swirling around that summer—his of a quizzical, yet calming and soothing nature; hers, deeply troubling and disturbing. Hilary had talked to Jimmy on the phone, giving him a bit of grief about doing so little to prepare for this trip. "Then he said, in really a puzzled way, 'You know, Mom, it's funny, but for some reason I just don't feel like I'm actually going to go on this trip.'"

A couple of days later, they talked again about his coming to our house before setting off on the adventure. He told her, "It's the strangest thing,

I find myself not worrying about everything, like I usually do. It feels really good!" For a month or so my wife had been feeling like something really big was about to happen, that the wheels were about to come off. She mentioned it to several friends; later they would remind her of those conversations.

The week before, we had gone to an outdoor Steely Dan concert at the Pala Indian reservation. Unlike her usually calm self, Hilary couldn't seem to sit still. "I'm going to get us something to drink," she said. As she waited in the concession line, she looked at the full moon just coming up. The words from the Creedence Clearwater Revival song, "Bad Moon Rising," filled her head, a warning not to come out tonight. After the concert, as we walked through the dark parking lot, Hilary shivered. "Something bad's coming. Jimmy feels better, but I feel worse."

I put my arm around her, hoping to soothe her.

The night before our hike, we had dinner with Laura, Anton, and their teenagers, Leo and Claire, at Fidel's, a very popular Mexican restaurant close by. Jimmy called to let us know he was stuck in traffic and would grab something to eat on the drive down from L.A. When Hilary, Brittany, and I got back to the house Jimmy was flopped on his favorite spot on the couch, watching the opening ceremonies of the Summer Olympics in Beijing.

As we watched the tiny teams from Uzbekistan and Kyrgyzstan stroll across the screen, we all wished that Ryan were here. He does a spot-on impression of Borat, Sasha Baron Cohen's character, that always left us rolling with hysterical laughter.

Jimmy got a call on his cell around ten and hopped up from the couch. "Some of my friends are in from New York and we're going to meet up at John and Hunter's. I'll see you guys later."

We knew "later" would be sometime in the wee hours. Before he bounded down the stairs and out the door, he kissed both Hilary and me and, wearing his beautiful smile, said, "Love you guys." He ran down the stairs.

We had barely gotten settled again when his head popped above the top step. "Britt, I really love Ryan. I'm so glad you married him." And with that, he was off.

The next morning I saw that his bed hadn't been slept in, so I assumed he'd stayed over with his friends. I hoped he'd get home soon. We would be leaving any minute to pick up Laura and her crew.

"Ready, honey?" I said to Hilary as I entered the living room.

"Sure. I've got some bottled water and snacks in the day pack." Trust Hilary to take care of the culinary needs of any adventure.

We gathered hats, packs, and anything else we might need on our hike in nearby Peñasquitos Canyon. Just as we started downstairs, the doorbell rang. Hilary followed as I went to answer it. Brittany was close behind.

A young deputy sheriff stood there, accompanied by a young Latino woman. "I'm from the Medical Examiner's office," she said. "May we come in?"

As I stepped aside to let them enter, I felt my life shattering.

~ 𝜚𝜚 ~

Five hours later we pulled up in front of the San Diego County Medical Examiner's office, a single-story cement block building built in the early 1970s. Anton drove as Hilary, Brittany, Laura, and I rode in silence, numb with shock and riddled with apprehension. We weren't supposed to be in a place that was off-limits to the bereaved, but as soon as the medical examiner and the deputy had left the house, I phoned my law partner, John Davies, to break the news. "John, something terrible's happened," I said, struggling not to cry. "Jimmy was hit by a car and killed early this morning."

Silence. Then a sharp intake of breath. "Jesus, Casey! What happened?"

"He decided to walk home from a friend's house. The road was dark. A driver didn't see him."

John was beyond devastated. Besides being one of my closest friends and mentor, he was the *unofficial* godfather to Brittany and Jimmy. I went on. "It gets worse. The medical examiner's office doesn't allow viewings. John, they won't let us see him! I *have* to see my boy!" My voice broke.

In many ways, John was the godfather to hundreds, if not thousands, of people in San Diego and throughout California. In his unassuming and behind-the-scenes manner, John Davies got things done—good things— and was one of the most politically connected people there was. "Let me see what I can do," he said and hung up.

Two hours later he called back. "I called Ron Roberts. He spoke with the M.E.'s office. They'll be expecting you at two-thirty."

"How can I ever thank you? You'll never know how important this is to me."

"Are you sure you want to see him? They told Ron he was badly beat up in the accident and ... you know what I'm trying to say."

"I've got to see him. I don't care what he looks like. He's still my son. We have to say goodbye." I thanked him again and hung up.

Now I looked at Hilary, sitting beside me in the back of Anton's rental car. She squeezed my hand, letting me know she was ready. I took a deep breath and opened the car door.

Chaplain Joe Davis stood on the steps of the entrance, waiting for us. His face reflected warmth, kindness, and compassion, exactly the qualities you hope to see in someone in his line of work. After we shook hands and introduced ourselves, Chaplain Davis led us into the building. His kind eyes told us he shared our sorrow as he said, "I've worked for several years as the chaplain for the M.E.'s office, assisting with the bereaved."

"On Saturdays?" I asked.

He shrugged and a small smile touched his lips. "Well, when a county supervisor calls... I'm glad to help you. Shall we pray?"

We joined hands and he spoke some beautiful words that I have no recollection of.

I cleared my throat, perhaps to rid it of the slightly medicinal smell that lingered in the hallway, perhaps to drive away the tears that had blocked it for the last half day. "So what happens next?" I asked.

He talked about selecting a mortuary, composing an obituary, applying for a death certificate—the cold, hard facts of the business of death. "And there will be an autopsy to determine if any drugs were involved."

Hilary turned to me, shock clear in her expression. Several of our friends had lost children to overdoses.

Joe seemed to sense her incredulity. He patted her shoulder. "I'm so sorry, but it's required." He turned to me. "Would you like to see Jimmy first?"

I could only nod. I gave Hilary and Brittany quick hugs and followed him down the drab, sterile hallway, our steps echoing from the linoleum. As we walked, he tried to prepare me. "So, as you know, we're not set up for viewings here. We're going into a small room around the corner. There will be a glass window. Jimmy will be lying on a gurney on the other side of the glass. He's in a large room where the, uh… recently deceased are examined. Lots of instruments, tables, and machines, but nobody else is in the room. The left side of his face is covered with scrapes from the road. I'll go in with you."

I took a deep breath as he led me into a five-by-five room. There was barely enough space for the two of us. And there was Jimmy on the other side of the glass. At least, it was Jimmy's body, but I instantly knew he wasn't there. He was already somewhere else. He was beautiful. His reddish brown hair, which usually flopped down over his forehead, was combed back, revealing that incredible face, the high cheekbones, long eyelashes, thin perfect lips, strong jaw and chin. His body was covered with a cream-colored blanket pulled up to his long neck. The left side of his face was toward the window, scraped and bruised, as I had been warned.

Later we would find out that around four-thirty that morning he had decided to walk home from his friend's house on the Del Dios Highway—Highway of the Gods—a dark, winding road with extremely narrow shoulders. The first car struck him at five-thirty a.m. It flipped over. The driver was fortunately unhurt. A few moments later another car blew through and struck Jimmy again. That car did not stop, and the driver never surfaced. Moments later the gods carried him away, leaving only this still-beautiful shell behind.

"Would you like to be alone?" the chaplain asked.

I nodded and he left, closing the door behind him. Words tumbled from me as tears streaked my face and dripped onto the floor. All the emotions I had experienced during his too-short lifetime as I watched him move from cradle to crib to dorm room and finally his own house overwhelmed me. This place of death was the last place I wanted to be and at the same time the only place I wanted to be. Chaplain Davis returned in a few minutes and took me back to the reception area. Hilary, Brittany, Laura, and Anton waited, pensive and anxious. Hilary and Brittany looked at me, imploring me to take away the horror, asking me silently to tell them that everything would be all right. I managed to speak. "I think you should see him. It will be okay."

I felt like an old hand at death as I prepared them for what they would see when the three of us walked into the viewing room.

That moment—that searing, electric moment—I can't tell you how proud I am of my wife and daughter and the courage they summoned to walk into that room. And I know we all felt it was very important for us to be there—to see Jimmy. Of that we have no doubts, no regrets.

After we said our goodbyes, Joe Davis escorted Laura and Anton down the hall to see Jimmy. The chaplain came right back, alone, and sat down with us. If possible, he became even more serious. He reached for Hilary's and my hands. "I have to tell you something," he said. "The journey you began only a few hours ago is one of the hardest there is. Losing a child is utterly devastating, and your marriage and relationship are going to be severely tested. The statistics are not good. Over fifty percent of couples who lose a child will divorce or separate within the first two years."

Hilary and I looked at each other, searching each other's eyes for any sign of doubt or fear. I found none in her. I looked into my heart and knew that we wouldn't be one of those statistics.

Chaplain Davis went on. "You will have to work incredibly hard to be there for one another, support each other, love each other, stay together. Whatever you do, stay together. I will pray that you do."

Hilary squeezed my hand in a silent promise: Forever and always.

MY FIRST ANGEL

EASTER, 1971. JUST a routine break from college. I'd gone up to Los Altos in northern California to spend it with my aunt and uncle, Joan and Stan Case, and their four kids. My mother and Laura had driven over from Springville in central California, checking out places to live. My USC roommate, another Stan, had also come home to the Bay Area, so I wasn't surprised when he called.

"Hey, Casey, Robin and I are going out tonight. You want to be Hilary Tedrow's date?"

No need to ask who he meant. If you were a male with a pulse at USC you knew who Hilary Tedrow was. For the last several months I'd been a "hasher" at the Delta Gamma house, dishing up food for the sorority women, and whenever I caught a glimpse of Hilary, I knew exactly why frat boys referred to her as a goddess. Man, was she hot!

Of course, even though I was drooling all over the phone, I tried to sound cool. "Sure. Why not?" I said.

"Uh, you know she's pinned to that Kappa Alpha guy?" Stan said.

"The guy who could double for Robert Redford? Sure, I know. But we're just out for a good time, right?"

Stan's relief was plain as he replied, "Right! See you about eight."

To be honest, if I'd passed up this opportunity to spend a couple of hours breathing the same air as Hilary Tedrow, my fraternity brothers would have kicked me out of the house.

I spent the afternoon dreaming about the date and fretting over what to wear and which cologne to put on. She'd been Senior Prom Queen at Menlo Atherton High School in 1968 and in November 1970 was crowned USC's Helen of Troy, to the surprise of no one except her. Being Helen of Troy was like homecoming queen and prom queen times a hundred, but it was far more than just a beauty pageant. The winner's duties included meeting with alumni groups all over the country, recruiting high school applicants and interfacing between faculty and students. With a hundred other girls in the running, she figured she had no chance of winning. Was she surprised when her name was announced!

I suppose I had casually mentioned to my family that I was going out with the current reigning Helen of Troy that night, and my mother and uncle, both USC alums, were very impressed. The doorbell rang and I hurried to answer it. By the time I got it open, my entire family had crowded close behind me, eager to get a glimpse of the goddess.

"Come on in," I said, standing aside.

Of course, all eight of the goons had to shout, "Hi!"

The volume and enthusiasm stopped Hilary in her tracks. Talk about an awkward moment. My ten-year-old cousin, Tom, saved the day. He pointed at Robin, then Hilary, and asked in a voice that would have done a ring announcer proud, "Hey, Casey, which one do you get?"

My face flamed as laughter engulfed the group. If I hadn't been a mature college man, I'd have pasted Tom a good one. Then I saw Hilary's eyes sparkling as she gave me a sideways glance and forgave the little imp. I made introductions and managed to get us out of there without too much interrogation from my support group.

Hilary drove and I sat next to her as Stan and Robin cuddled in the back seat. We made small talk as we headed across the bay to Berkeley. She parked close to a busy pub near the UC campus and we went in. Pitchers of beer came and went as we talked and laughed. I couldn't stop looking at her as she tucked her long brown hair behind her ears. Her high cheekbones suggested her Czech heritage. Every time she smiled her killer smile, dimples dented her cheeks and her bright, brown, inviting eyes shone. Her voice was a whiskey-and-cigarettes whisper, earthy, evocative, sexy. But more than just beautiful, she was the most extraordinarily beautiful human being I'd ever met. How could someone so physically attractive be so humble, caring, smart, sweet, and genuinely nice? Whenever the conversation centered on her, she turned it away from herself and encouraged us to talk.

At one point, Stan and I went to the men's room. "So how's it going?" he asked as we stood at urinals.

"You talking about peeing?" I asked, making sure I was hitting where I was aiming.

"No, you idiot! With Hilary."

"Man, she's wonderful. Too bad she's pinned to that KA," I replied, tucking and zipping.

Stan smirked as he finished and said, "Robin told me that's over."

I swear Carole King began to sing in the men's room at that moment, because I felt the earth move under my feet.

After we left the pub we went to the Claremont Hotel in nearby Piedmont, where Stan had grown up. "We used to slide down that hill behind the hotel on blocks of ice we 'borrowed' from refrigerated trucks." Stan smiled reminiscently.

"Sounds like fun," I said.

We looked at each other and grinned. The back door of the hotel kitchen was open, so he and I "borrowed" a couple of large silver serving trays.

The grass was moist with evening dew and we took turns sitting on the trays and sliding down the hill, shrieking with laughter. When the trays hit dry spots, the abrupt halt pitched us off our makeshift sleds, causing us to tumble and roll several more yards, whooping and hollering, until hotel security showed up.

We dashed into the darkness and dove into Hilary's car, our clothes soaked and covered with grass stains, still grinning and screeching like hyenas. We dropped Stan and Robin off and headed back across the bay. I offered to drive, and Hilary fell asleep next to me. The lights lulled me, and my thoughts drifted back to just before Christmas. It had been only four months since the police had knocked on our wreath-bedecked door to tell us of my father's death. As I glanced at Hilary's peaceful face, joy and longing overwhelmed me. *How is it possible*, I wondered, *that a few short months can hold both the worst day and the best day of my life?*

⁓ 🙢🙠 ⁓

Easter Break over, I went back to school, living proof of all the clichés about love that have made their way into popular culture: bolt of lightning, love at first sight, head over heels. I went over to the Delta Gamma house and asked for Hilary. It took her only a few seconds to come down from her room.

"Would you like to go to the Delt party next weekend?" I asked.

"Yes," she said. That one word was enough.

A week after the party, we went with some other couples to The Luau, a very popular Polynesian-themed restaurant/bar in West Los Angeles that specialized in Mai Tais, Fog Cutters, Lava Flows, and other complicated, rum-based concoctions. A miniature tropical island at sunset with sand, palm trees, and waterfalls had been re-created along one wall. A soundtrack of breaking waves, rustling palm fronds, ukulele, and slide guitar made us feel like we were in paradise. Hilary and I strolled over and, sipping something that featured an umbrella, began to fantasize.

"What if we were the only ones on that island?" I said

"What if we had to stay there forever?" she replied.

"I'd go fishing every day."

"We'd build a hut from palm fronds."

"We'd be as brown as our hair." By now, we were giggling and grinning. We reached out at the same time and held hands.

We were virtually inseparable during the rest of the semester. I was surrendering to this pure, blinding light that had enveloped me. There wasn't one ounce of doubt in my mind that God had sent me an angel, and her name was Hilary Tedrow. I desperately hoped this wasn't too good to be true.

Hilary and I finished our final exams and went off to our summer jobs, she to Corona del Mar, where she would serve hungry customers at Zubie's Pizza Kitchen, and I to Honolua, Maui, to pick pineapples from the land that is now the Kapilua Resort. At least every other day, I wrote to Hilary.

The days I received her reply were red-letter days. Fortunately there were a lot of them. Over the first month, mine were mostly travelogues: work, the beauty of Maui, surfing, skin-diving, bagging rays. Insipid and boring. That changed the first week in July when she sent me a scathing letter that is forever burned into my brain.

"You are an emotionless shell," she wrote. "If you have feelings you certainly don't show them. Are we just pen pals? If so, tell me."

I felt like I'd been punched in the stomach. How could she have gotten me so wrong? Had I just lost the best thing that had ever happened to me? The next day I composed a four-page letter. "Hilary, you are not a pen pal. You are not a friend. You're the girl that I love. I must be crazy for not writing every day and telling you that. When I get home I want you to be there—I want to hold you, see you every minute. I need your warmth, your voice, your spirit. But maybe I'm too late in telling you how I feel. Please give me a chance."

She did. Thank God! I received many wonderful letters from Hilary and wrote back many more to her, opening my heart. I never mentioned my dad in my letters, but I thought about him every day. The pain seemed to have receded, and I didn't feel as frightened.

More than the letters changed. One day, close to sunset, I was working in a field on a high hill, pulling pineapples from their leafy bases. I paused and looked over the deep blue waters of Molokai and for the first time in seven months I thought, "This is good. I feel good. I think I'm going to be okay."

And I was.

JIMMY

"I'LL NEVER MAKE any money!" he bellowed to the driver. He was sitting, as usual, in the back seat, dressed in a sport coat, white shirt, and club tie, with his briefcase on the seat next to him. His longish strawberry-blond hair had fallen over his ever-perspiring brow. He was slightly pudgy, but not overweight. He began to sob.

The driver glanced at him in the rearview mirror and asked, "Why are you crying?"

"Because I don't know how to do anything! How am I going to get a job when I don't know how to do anything?"

As she slowed for a red light, the driver struggled to suppress a smile. She turned and looked over the seat. "Jimmy, you're only four years old. You don't have to worry about getting a job. That's years away, honey." The light changed and Hilary continued down the street to Jimmy's pre-school, with him still fretting about his inability to hold down a job. It was December 1987.

Since the day he was born, November 8, 1983, James Tedrow Gauntt seemed to be driven, as if there was so much he had to wring out of life, that he was behind already. He walked at nine months, eager to be on his own. He loved baseball and, growing tired of me reading to him the San Diego Padres box scores in the sports section of the newspaper, he pretty much taught himself to read by the age of five so he could look them up himself.

Nobody was harder on Jimmy than Jimmy. I remember a parent-teacher conference soon after he started the first grade. When the teacher asked if there was anything she should know about Jimmy, Hilary said, "Don't let him take himself too seriously. He will want to learn everything fast and get on to the next thing. Let him know it's okay to relax and just have some fun."

As a toddler, Jimmy's uniform was sweatshirt, sweatpants, and cowboy boots. He didn't care if the summer sun or winter rains beat down. Sweats and boots were his go-to, always.

He'd race around, pedaling his Hot Wheels tricycle as hard as he could. He was constantly falling and crashing, and his face, knees, elbows—every exposed surface—bore the scabs, scars, and bruises of his escapades. A permanent sheen of perspiration covered his face and dampened his hair with an earthy musk fragrance.

By age four, Jimmy graduated from sweats to "office" clothes. He wanted to dress like his dad, the lawyer. Every morning we'd shave together. He'd perch on a stool beside me at the vanity. I would lather his face and mine with my shaving brush and Old Spice soap. Then I'd hand him one of my extra razors, *sans* blade. I had a hard time keeping a straight face as he mimicked my every move, scraping off the lather and rinsing his razor. Then I would pour a miniscule amount of aftershave into his tiny palm and he'd rub it over his face with such energy that I wondered if his emerging freckles would be scrubbed away.

Hilary had bought him a small plastic briefcase to carry his ever-expanding cache of football and baseball cards and a pad of paper and pens I had given him. When he was decked out in his business togs, he reminded us of Pee Wee Herman, from one of Jimmy's favorite TV shows, *Pee Wee's Playhouse*. For Jimmy's fourth birthday party, Jim Blackburn, one of our good friends, came over dressed as Pee Wee and entertained Jimmy and his friends. He was the hit of the party, at least in Jimmy's eyes.

Jimmy always seemed older than his age. He thought older. He was more in tune with things and others around him. It's funny, but I don't remember him as a baby. I remember him as older, more mature, and having these grown-up conversations with him when he was really little. He had an acute sensitivity to others and their feelings, and what they did to others and what others did to him.

He was very secure with his intelligence but he never used it to show off or make someone feel small. He had to learn and had to do well in school; he demanded it. His teachers loved him for it, this enthusiastic kid with an unquenchable thirst for knowledge.

Jimmy was a sweet kid. He got along with everybody, meeting each person young or old, with equanimity and respect. He also loved to cuddle with me and Hilary, but most especially his mother.

There were a couple of years, somewhere around fifth or sixth grade, where practically every night Jimmy would get out of bed and come to our room. He'd had a bad dream, or heard a sound, or wasn't feeling well. He'd drag in a blanket and pillow and curl up on the floor at the foot of our bed. After a while we set up a bed of blankets and pillows for him. We called it "camping out." He said it made him feel better hearing us breathe.

Like his older sister, Jimmy was a good kid, never got into trouble, and had a very firm stance on what was right and wrong. He was a borderline Goody Two-shoes.

This created some difficulty when he entered junior high. Seventh grade was a huge transition from a handful of eager teachers who treated him like one of their own children to a multitude of instructors who had probably hung on more than a few years too long; a small, cozy class of best friends to a huge slug of strange faces. A number of his close friends were entering puberty or getting close, and were bigger and more attractive to the girls. They were starting to surf and skate and get into a little trouble. Jimmy was a late bloomer like me and as he grew distant from his elementary school friends, he seemed in danger of turning into a loner.

Brittany, a junior in high school at the time, finally intervened. She went to John Dudek, an eighth-grader who was the brother of her best friend and like a big brother to Jimmy, as well as a stud in junior high. Brittany implored John to look after Jimmy, and he did. He checked on Jimmy between classes, and if anyone glanced cross-eyed at Jimmy, John warned them with a look. By the time Jimmy entered eighth grade, enough of John's coolness had rubbed off on him and he was back in the fold with friends and even a few girls.

Jimmy was as dedicated to sports as he was to books and learning. At six, he insisted on playing T-ball, a low-stress, fun precursor to baseball. He moved on to Little League, and I managed his team, the Giants, when he was eleven. Jimmy pitched and played third base. He was one of the best kids on the team, winning the Best Sport award when he was ten. He worked hard to win, and very early on looked after his teammates. Were they having fun? Were they getting enough playing time? He showed a remarkable ability to tune into others' emotions, just like his big sister.

Once, after a rare loss, I scolded the team. "You aren't trying hard enough. You've got to give it everything you've got." I happened to be looking at Jimmy when I said it. He was silent as we drove home. When I opened the front door, he stormed past me, slamming the door to his room.

When Hilary went to call him for dinner, he shouted through the closed door, "I don't want any!"

"I think he's crying," she said as she came back to the kitchen.

I figured maybe losing the game had upset him and that he'd get over it after he got it out of his system. "He'll come out when he's ready. Or when he gets hungry."

Two hours later, he was still holed up. I went to his room, knocked, and entered. He was lying face down on the top bunk, still wearing his uniform and cleats. "Hey, son, you missed dinner."

He glared at me. Then for the first and only time, he yelled at me. "Dad, don't ever tell me I don't try hard enough! I always try hard in everything I do! You know that!"

Surprised by his fury, I replied, "I wasn't yelling at you. I was just trying to make a point with the whole team."

"But you looked right at me."

"Son, I'm sorry. I didn't mean to hurt you." I held out my arms. It took him about three seconds to throw himself at me. That hug set things right and we were friends once more.

Jimmy hustled. He was small for his age, but he played every sport he tried with a big heart and an intensity that made him the coaches' favorite.

I remember both of his home runs in Little League, the buzzer-beating, game-winning, long-range shot in a junior high basketball game, his first touchdown as wide receiver as a senior in high school and being named the San Diego *Union-Tribune's* player of the week for amassing 130 receiving yards. I watched in awe as the 18-year-old cleared six feet two inches in the high jump, three inches above his height.

Jimmy loved school, as did Brittany, although I never lectured or used trips to the seamy side of town to stress the importance of education. I'd had enough of that from my father. I wasn't going to visit his "sins" upon my offspring. Because I loved my job as a lawyer and did well at it, they absorbed the idea that I had gotten where I was because I did well in school. I didn't need to hammer it into them.

I liked the quiet solitude of studying, and being able to figure things out, and to write something well. I wanted to do well in school to please my parents, but I did it as much for myself as for them. I liked it, I worked hard at it, and I expected to be appropriately recognized for it.

Jimmy's peers recognized his hard work, too. He was president of his senior class, wore his homecoming prince crown proudly, and delivered the morning announcements over the school P.A. system. Jimmy also discovered theatre his senior year and played minor roles in two plays. That bug bit him good.

Jimmy's 4.65 grade point average, a full year's worth of college credits, and his leadership skills made his admission to USC as a full-ride Trustee Scholar practically a slam dunk. This made the old man proud; I, too, had been a Trustee Scholar at SoCal.

One weekend in September 2003, I drove up to Los Angeles to visit Jimmy. He was a sophomore, majoring in Spanish. He had spent the summer in Madrid, living with a family and taking some Spanish literature classes at a nearby university affiliated with USC. Jimmy, his Sigma Alpha Epsilon pledge brother, Kelly Jiménez, and Steven Tran, a close friend of Jimmy's from high school, were renting a dilapidated bungalow built in the 1920s on 32nd Street in back of the Shrine Auditorium. Even though he was president of his fraternity pledge class, he couldn't live in the frat house. "It's like living in an insane asylum. I need someplace quiet to work on my writing," he said.

Sunday morning Jimmy and I had breakfast at the infamous Pantry on Olympic at Figueroa, and then went on a hike in the San Gabriel Mountains. It was a spectacularly clear day with hot Santa Ana winds blowing in from the desert to the east. As we hiked the dry, dusty trails, Jimmy's voice rose, his eyes sparkled, and his hands flew as he told me his idea for a play he wanted to write for Introduction to Playwriting, a class he had added at the last minute.

"Dad, I read something recently about anopheles mosquitoes. The females are the only ones that bite. The males are smaller but have huge reproductive organs making up a third of their body weight. The males are obsessively devoted to the females, although dominated like slaves. So I have this idea about a guy who is quarantined in a hospital room and two mosquitoes are in there with him, a male and a female. He's tormented by these insects and begins to fanaticize about the female. The female, 'Ana,' is transformed into a bombshell of a woman with red hair, wearing a leather dominatrix outfit, and the guy falls in love with her. I'll have a saxophone make the buzzing sounds and a jazz band will play smoking-hot music throughout the play. What do you think?"

I thought Jimmy was destined to be a writer, regardless of what anyone else thought he "could" or "should" otherwise be doing. He never had to speculate or worry about what Hilary and I thought of this path he had chosen.

As we hiked, I remembered an e-mail he had sent me back in early February. He'd been writing a paper on James Joyce's book, *A Portrait of the Artist as a Young Man.* The book deals with a son's relationship to his father and his resistance to his father's influence. After fleeing from his father, he realizes that he has become all that he hated about his father.

Words from Jimmy's e-mail floated into my head. "I feel so damn lucky to be your son. So many of the things I love about myself are such reflections of you. You have given me such freedom to find myself. And I know that that is a unique occurrence among father-son relationships. Thank you, thank you, thank you. I will make you proud. I will make *us* proud.

"Love, Jim"

At that moment on the trail it began to really sink in that Jimmy was far more creative and imaginative than I had realized. I could see the wheels spinning a thousand miles an hour in his head. He was beginning to explore and soar with his writing. It didn't quite register with me at the time—I mean, I didn't come up with the words to describe who and what I was seeing and hearing—but here before me on the trail, throwing ideas back at me over his shoulder, was an emerging artist.

We walked and talked for the next two hours about the play. He got me completely caught up in it. I was so happy that he was opening up and sharing this with me, giving me a glimpse into how his amazing mind worked. I watched as he began the climb out of the skin that used to be Jimmy and transform into the person he was destined to become, possessed of boundless energy and unabashed and courageous in creativity and passion. I had the privilege on that trail of bearing witness to the gigantic leap he was taking in his life, from which he never looked back.

Four months later, Hilary, Jimmy, and I went to the South Rim of the Grand Canyon to celebrate my fifty-fourth birthday. We stayed at the historic El Tovar hotel, which sits directly on the canyon rim. We had adjoining rooms, more like a suite, separated by a glass door. Not a lot of privacy.

That first night I got up to pee around three a.m. I looked through the glass partition into Jimmy's room and saw a bluish-green glow emanating from his bed. Jimmy had booted up his laptop, and I knew he was working on that play. He saw me peering in at him and he gave a little wave. I pointed at my watch. He just smiled and went back to work.

Jimmy worked feverishly on his project, leaving it only to eat or hike. Midway through one of our rambles along the canyon rim, Jimmy excused himself. "Just got a brainstorm," he said. "Gotta get it down before I forget it."

We watched him lope back to the room, awed by his enthusiasm, but there was also an undercurrent of concern about how frenetic he was about this project. It wasn't the first time nor would it be the last we saw Jimmy throw himself like that into his writing, or a sport, or a girl. There was an intensity, an urgency, an immediacy.

SAX MAN

JIMMY CAME BY his love of music naturally. Growing up, music was my passion, second only to golf. As a six-year-old during our first summer in Itasca, the Chicago suburb where I grew up, I hung out a lot at the country club swimming pool. One of the lifeguards had a ukulele and would play during his breaks. I'll admit I idolized this tall, muscular, young virtuoso. He taught me a few chords and simple songs. The uke was perfect for my small hands, and after much begging, my mother bought me my own. I'd play for hours, practicing the songs I'd learned at lessons, and then experimenting and exploring with my own made-up chords and songs.

At the end of Sunday school class at the First Presbyterian Church, we'd assemble and sing several hymns. I loved to figure out and sing the harmonies, and I wasn't a bashful singer. I sang loudly and took the lead every chance I had, singing solos in several school plays and recitals.

In the 1950s, Mitch Miller invited us to sing along by following the bouncing ball over the lyrics of the songs that scrolled across our tiny black-and-white TV. Then came *Hootenanny*, and the airwaves were filled with folk music. The banjo was a featured instrument with folk groups like the Kingston Trio. I quickly jumped on that bandwagon and bought a banjo and took several lessons. Just as I was nearing proficiency on the thing, the Beatles showed up. I can still remember the first time I heard "I Want to

Hold Your Hand." I instantly realized that all of the music I'd listened to during the past thirteen years was total crap. I was completely taken over by their tight harmonies, the driving beat with Motown undertones, their attitude, their bad-boy look. The Monday after the Beatles appeared for the first time on the Ed Sullivan TV show, my buddy Jerry Englebrook and I bought Beatle wigs—the hair was a shocking one-half inch over our ears. We wore them to school the next day. The wigs were confiscated by our principal, Miss Brooks, and we got detentions. North School did not tolerate subversive activity.

On the heels of the Beatles came the Rolling Stones, Hollies, Byrds, Yardbirds, The Who, The Animals, The Lovin' Spoonful, Buffalo Springfield, Herman's Hermits, Paul Revere's Raiders—the list goes on and on. I was smack in the middle of the golden age of music and loved every second of it. The banjo went into the closet. My ukulele snapped in half when I sat on my bed, forgetting that it was buried under the covers. It was time to move on.

Not long after I started my sophomore year some friends and I decided to form a garage band called the Whatzit Four. Drummer Roger Holmes drove the beat while Mike Sims' lead guitar wailed as he sang. Wayne Paney, my gymnastics teammate, strummed rhythm guitar. I thumped away on my self-taught electric bass and sang lead. A few months later, Greg DeBruyne joined on keyboards, and we became the Whatzit Four (+ One).

We practiced for hours, and as soon as we had a couple of sets of covers under our belts, we started playing parties in town. By our junior year we were working big dances at Lake Park and other local high schools, as well colleges in the Chicago area.

I went crazy and let my flattop grow out a couple of inches, horrifying my parents and coaches. My parents cautioned me against long hair, drugs, girls, and dropping out of school. All I wanted was girls, fame, and riches. We struck a deal: I could play in a band as long as I bought my own gear.

For frugal me, money was no object as I went in search of girls, fame, girls, riches, and girls.

—⁂—

Jimmy was in the fourth grade when one day a musical instrument company demonstrated a bunch of instruments and let the kids try them, the aim being to hook the parents into renting an instrument for their fledgling virtuoso. When Jimmy came home, he was so excited that he could hardly talk when he announced to Hilary, "I want to play the saxophone!" He handed her the price list and, of course, the sax, at twenty-eight dollars a month, was one of the most expensive instruments to rent.

Hilary scanned the list and, hoping to negotiate a lesser price, inquired, "Jimmy, what about the flute or the clarinet?"

"No! The saxophone!"

Hilary sighed. *Well, he'll try it for a month, tops, and we won't have to shell out for long,* she thought.

Jimmy began taking weekly lessons at the Boys and Girls Club across the street from school from a nice young man fresh out of college. Hilary's hopes of a minimal investment dwindled as one month extended into two, then six, then a year.

And Jimmy practiced—a lot. Occasionally I would run into his room because I swear it sounded like he had strung one of our cats up by its hind legs. The screeches slowly became notes and then recognizable songs. We realized that Jimmy was serious, so we purchased the sax we'd been renting. His instructor moved away soon after Jimmy started fifth grade, and Hilary called a music store in Encinitas to inquire about teachers and lessons.

The proprietor said, "Well, we have this older gentleman, Anthony Ortega, who is really good. He's like a grandfather to his students. Very patient. But he's on vacation so if you want to get started right away we have another young teacher available."

"Thanks, but I think we'll wait for Mr. Ortega to get back," she said, making one of the best decisions she ever made, both for Jimmy's musical career and his life.

For eight years, Anthony Ortega tutored Jimmy in the technique, tone, and art of playing the saxophone. Tony was one of the top jazz sax men in the country—or the world—probably best known in Paris, where he lived and played for many years after World War II. By the time we met him, Tony was in his seventies, still playing gigs and recording.

In 1999, when Jimmy was a sophomore at Torrey Pines High School, Tony helped Hilary and me to select a "gently used" but high-end alto saxophone manufactured by the Henri Selmer Company of France. For three years, Tony, Jimmy, and that sax were inseparable.

During his senior year, Jimmy and his fellow classmates were awash in the college application process. One of the assignments in his AP English class was to put together a personal statement, a requirement for most college applications. Jimmy wrote, "Welcome Home, Henri," in which it isn't revealed until the end that Henri is his saxophone. His teacher found it so exemplary that she read it to the class. When she had finished, Chris Santore, one of Jimmy's classmates and a good friend, leaned over to another student and said, "Shit! We're never getting into college."

When Jimmy graduated, Tony gave Jimmy a handmade leather saxophone strap for Henri. On the inside of the instrument's neck brace, he'd used a wood-burning tool to engrave *Jimmy Gauntt June 2002 Success to You Always Anthony Ortega*.

Only years later would we realize how this first "Henry" influenced Jim. He would use that name for the main characters in two of his screenplays: Henry Allman in *The Leather Clad Chaperone* (the play about the smokin'-hot mosquito that he pitched to me on the hiking trail) and Henry Torrid in *Now's The Time,* a screenplay about a young sax player struggling to make it in the Los Angeles music scene in the late 1960s. "Now's The Time" was also one of Jimmy's favorite tunes by legendary jazz sax man Charlie Parker. Tony taught Jimmy how to play it. Another Henry, Jimmy's friend from high school, would be the last person to see him alive.

Tony was much more than a music teacher to our son. He was Jimmy's bridge and guide to the realm of art and creativity. He deeply inspired Jimmy to find and pursue his passion. Jimmy said it best in this letter he wrote to Tony when he was a freshman at the University of Southern California.

"Dear Tony, I'm sitting in my dorm room listening to your album, *On Evidence.* High school seems like a very long time ago now. I already have a hard time remembering classes, teachers, people. But what is so close to me still, what I remember so well, are the Thursday afternoons I spent with you. I'm taking a class right now about the development of the artist, the characteristics of the artist, the personality of the artist. A lot of the kids think the artist is someone separate, foreign, an unfriendly figure writing from the shadows about things no one else can see. But I know they're wrong. I know an artist. I know you.

"The artist I know is brilliant. He shares that moment when the soul steps in front of the mind, and hidden places of beauty that he never knew were inside of him are uncovered. I will always be your student; you will always be my teacher. You will always be the artist I know.

Forever fortunate to know you,

Forever in gratitude,

Forever in love.

Your student and friend,

Jimmy Gauntt"

This letter came into our lives just two days before Jimmy's memorial service on August 15, 2008. My cousin, Diana, went to Tony's house to break the news of Jimmy's death to him and his wife, Mona, and to ask Tony if he would play at Jimmy's service. The news hit eighty-year-old Tony hard. As Diana was leaving, he said, "Wait a minute." He left and returned a few moments later with the above letter. "I think Jimmy's folks would like to have this," he said as he handed it to her.

John Davies, our "godfather," used his tenure as Chair of the University of California's Board of Regents to pave the way for the first memorial service ever held in the Mandeville Auditorium on the UC San Diego campus. A thousand bereft souls gathered for the service.

Jimmy's brother-in-law, Ryan, read that letter. Then he honored Jimmy and us with his memoriam, a work of art, opening with these lines.

"F. Scott Fitzgerald once wrote, 'For a while after you read John Keats all other poetry seems to be only whistling or humming.' The same can be said for a person having the privilege of being in the presence of James 'Jimmy' Tedrow Gauntt. No one else was as bright, as talented, as kind, as genuine, or as loving. Jimmy was music, the rest of us mere explanation of its sound."

Tony played Parker's "Now's The Time," plus an original composition for Jimmy and a very moving, soulful, rendition of "Amazing Grace."

The day after Jimmy died, Hilary, Brittany, Ryan, and I took a walk along the edge of the San Elijo Lagoon near our house to get some fresh air and to steal a few moments away from the calls, the flower deliveries, and the pathetically sad eyes of those who dropped by. We needed to clear our heads and slip into the eye of our hurricane, if for only a moment.

As we wandered along the trail, Ryan volunteered to write Jimmy's obituary. I was relieved because neither Hilary nor I was able to construct a coherent sentence, much less attempt to summarize his life without completely breaking down. Hilary and Brittany made three decisions that set the course of how we would mourn the loss of our son and brother.

Our house was already overflowing with floral tributes. "How about in the obituary we say, 'Instead of flowers, please make a donation to After-School All-Stars'?" I suggested, naming a charity I used to chair and for which Brittany and Jimmy had both interned.

Brittany stopped short. "No. We will set up a fund at Torrey Pines High School in Jimmy's memory and award scholarships to seniors who pursue studies in the arts, music, literature, and theatre. That's what Jimmy would want us to do." During the next few weeks, more than $100,000 would be contributed to the James T. Gauntt Memorial Scholarship Fund at Torrey Pines High School.

Hilary said with even more conviction, "We cannot let Jimmy's death take us down. That would be the worst thing we could do to him. He only ever wanted to make us happy. We have to survive this for him." We sealed our pact with an embrace.

We couldn't bear the thought of going to a cemetery to visit Jimmy, so Hilary came up with the idea to place a memorial bench along one of the trails at the lagoon where we could come and commune with Jimmy. Nine months and a significant donation to the Lagoon Conservancy later, Jimmy's Bench came to be.

We struggled with the appropriate words to inscribe on the bench— perhaps something from Shakespeare or Tennyson, two of Jimmy's favorites? But nothing seemed quite right.

And then Hilary had an epiphany. "Why don't we use something from our favorite writer?"

Perfect.

The penultimate three lines of Jimmy's letter to his old friend are engraved on Jimmy's memorial bench at the San Elijo Lagoon.

Forever Fortunate To Know You, Forever In Gratitude, Forever In Love.
11/83 Jimmy Gauntt 8/08

THE ROLEX

I T WAS A Thursday afternoon and I had come home early from work as I'd done each day since I'd gone back to the firm a month ago. I could focus for only about four hours in the morning on my law practice before heading home, exhausted, to be with Hilary. I'd gone into Jimmy's bedroom every day, sorting through his drawers, closets, and bookshelves. Half-filled boxes held the things he would not need again: clothing, books, miscellaneous odds and ends, waiting to be stored in the third-floor attic. Even though he hadn't lived here for six years, it remained "Jimmy's room."

I'd done a little bit each day, my limit. Neither Hilary nor I wanted to erase Jimmy from the room, only to soften his overwhelming presence.

As I pored through thousands of his football, basketball, and baseball cards, I felt long-repressed anger bubbling up. My mother had tossed my card collection after I left for college. A fortune had surely been lost by her unthinking cleaning. I shrugged, dismissing the angst. I hadn't been even close to the collector Jimmy was. I got into them for the bubble gum.

Memories spiraled through the room as I packed ribbons, medals, and trophies for races won, teams joined, most improved, best sport; we'd saved them all. Folders full of notes and essays made me want to read them, and I promised myself that someday I would. I kept sorting. Holding his diplomas, report cards, photographs of friends, crushes, and happy times made me smile yet want to weep for all he'd accomplished in such a short life. Sifting through the drawers of his desk was like an archeological dig—layer upon layer of the things important to him, each older than the one pressing down from above.

And his books. The books. Jimmy had hundreds of books in his room. His cabin in Laurel Canyon had even more, but none of us had been able to face going up there to clean it out yet. It was easier to just pay the rent, put off the pain. Going through his titles made me feel—well—lazy. The bookcases held everything written by Shakespeare, Joyce, Tolstoy, London, Keats, Tennyson, Whitman, Hemingway, Updike, Kesey, Steinbeck, and all of the heavyweights in Spanish literature—in Spanish. Some of them were the books my friends and I were forced to read in high school and college, presumably to broaden our perspectives and become conversant with great literature.

The tomes that left many of us scrambling for Cliff Notes, Jimmy read voluntarily. He actually kept a reading list throughout high school and college that he'd plow through during summer breaks and downtime in the school year. I opened a few at random. Margins were filled with notes in his undecipherable squiggle, and the dog-eared pages showed signs of heavy use. Not for Jimmy a quick perusal and off to something else. He worked these masterpieces and they worked him. Sometimes I'd had the urge to hide the latest bestseller that I was reading, afraid that Jimmy would scoff. But that wasn't his style. He was so engaged in his own life he didn't waste time trying to run anyone else's.

Shortly after he had graduated from college, he told Hilary, "I wonder about all the books in the libraries all over the world. Millions of books. And I think to myself, 'Look at all of the books that have been written. It can't be that hard to write a book. Wouldn't it be cool to go to a library and see the binding of a book with the name Jimmy Gauntt on it?'"

—⚭⚭—

His backpack still lay where he'd tossed it not that many Fridays ago. I hadn't had the heart, or the stomach, to touch it. Inside were the things he thought about that late Friday afternoon, almost the last things he touched. They were a thread to him, a piece of the grand mosaic that was him. Opening it would invade his privacy and the space that was his sanctuary. There were lots of reasons and excuses to not open that pack, but eventually I did.

Inside, on top, was a ball of clothing, including a pair of well-worn blue jeans, a couple of dark T-shirts, some boxer shorts that appeared to be clean, and a rumpled dress shirt and slacks. Knowing Jimmy, he surely would have attempted to wear them as-is to the Saturday dinner with Laura, Anton, and his cousins. There were no socks, swim trunks, or tennis shorts. He'd borrow—he would have borrowed—some of mine. The rest of the pack was filled with books I'd never heard of.

Buried in one of the pouches was a receipt dated May 24, 2008, for $7.87 from Roberto's Mexican take-out in Solana Beach. Three rolled tacos, one bean burrito, and a small beverage. I flashed back to Jimmy's memorial service. One of his oldest and best friends, Erik Shepner, composed himself at the podium and began. "I used to dream, literally dream, that one day I would have the chance to get on a stage and sing Jimmy's praises. It's unfortunate that it is a setting like this, but it is one of the greatest honors of my life. The last time I saw Jimmy was a couple of months ago at Roberto's in Solana Beach. We had a great talk and he seemed really well… he was just on it. And his parting words as we were leaving, the last thing he said, was, 'Shep. Write me something beautiful. I want you to write something beautiful and send it to me.' And I said, 'Yeah, Jim. I will.' I didn't get the chance until now. So I wrote something which I hope is beautiful."

I wondered if this receipt was from the last time he and Erik saw each other, the night Jimmy asked Shep to write him something beautiful, a request that inspired us to create the website www.WriteMeSomethingBeautiful.com.

In one of the front pockets of his jeans were some crumpled debit card receipts from a Quizno's on Sunset Boulevard, Santa Monica Liquor, and a Chevron station. In a back pocket were two ticket stubs for the ten-thirty p.m. showing of David Green's new film, *Pineapple Express,* at The Grove multiplex on Sunset Boulevard two nights before he came home. Who did he go with? A girl? I may never know.

After cleaning out the pack, I opened the top drawer of the nightstand next to Jimmy's king-sized bed for the first time. Nestled on top of the conglomeration of stuff that always seems to accumulate in such places, I found a watch, a Rolex Explorer. Definitely not the watch we had given him when he graduated from high school. We had never seen Jimmy wear this watch, and he had never mentioned it. In fact, he seldom wore a watch of any kind and never wore rings. Was it his? Where had he gotten it?

A stream of questions raced through my mind. When was the last time he wore it? When did he place it in the drawer? Was he wearing it when he came home that Friday? Had he taken it off and put it in the drawer before he left for the party? I had no answers. Maybe when Hilary came home she could shed some light on the mystery.

She and Jimmy had been so close, almost creepy close, always sitting next to each other on the couch, constantly holding hands or hugging. This went on for years. Once, when Jimmy was in his late teens and cuddling with Hilary, Brittany had exclaimed, "You guys shouldn't be doing that! It's weird." They just ignored her and continued loving and stroking each other, two halves of one heart.

Hilary had been my angel, my rock, after my dad died and then when Jimmy was killed, but now I was worried. She dragged around the house, reluctantly went grocery shopping—afraid of bumping into someone who hadn't heard the news, or worse, seeing a friend catch her eye and scurry away into another aisle. She moved through her days as though she were living on borrowed time. "I miss him so much! I just want to be with him," she'd say.

Her words snapped me out of my own pit of despair. Could she really mean that? What would I do if I lost the love of my life as well as my only son? How could Brittany and I survive if Hilary died of grief or, worse, took her life? Losing my dad had driven me to the brink of sanity; loving Hilary had brought me back. Without her, I, too, would die. I began to keep a close eye on her, trying to ease her pain and keep her anchored in life. I didn't know then that a medium and a miracle would change everything in just a few short months.

I took the watch upstairs to our bedroom and put it in a wooden jewelry box with a glass cover that I keep in our walk-in closet. The box contains a plastic bag holding Jimmy's wallet with the three twenty-dollar bills he was carrying that last night, his keys and his cell phone. The bits and pieces that the medical examiner had recovered from his body. Taking a deep breath, I closed the box and went downstairs.

The next day Tom Strickler drove down from Los Angeles to have dinner with Hilary, Brittany, Ryan, and me. Although we'd met Tom only once before, he was Jimmy's friend and wanted to be with us at this time to talk about Jimmy. As a founding partner of Endeavor, now William Morris Endeavor, one of the most powerful entertainment agencies in the country, Tom was a major force in Hollywood, with a triple A client list of writers, actors, and directors. Jimmy's very close friend, fraternity brother, and writing partner, Evan Nicholas, went to work for Endeavor as Tom's assistant right after college, and he had introduced Tom to Jimmy. We were amazed at Tom's courage in coming. Most of our friends were struggling with what to say in a sympathy card. Personal visits were not on their radar. We were like their kryptonite.

That evening we lost ourselves in Hilary's good food and good stories that brought laughter and tears to us all. One of the "Jimmy" stories Tom shared with us was about an article that appeared a year earlier in *Fade In*, a Hollywood magazine that caters to the film industry. It was a rather scathing and unflattering piece about Endeavor in general and Tom in particular. "Jimmy was the only person who ever said anything to me after it came out. Nobody else said a word. Not a co-worker, client, colleague—nobody. Everyone in my business reads that rag religiously, so I knew that practically everybody I know read that article. Yet Jimmy was the only one who had the balls to bring it up." He blinked away tears. "He was a good friend."

When dinner was almost over, Tom said, "I hope this doesn't come off as petty or materialistic, but I need to ask you something. A few weeks after last year's L.A. Marathon I gave Jimmy a watch to commemorate our achievement and friendship. I was curious if you've come across it. I've been worried that Jimmy may have left it in his place at Laurel Canyon or it might have 'wandered off.'"

"Excuse me," I said, laying aside my napkin. "I'll be right back." I returned moments later and handed Tom the Rolex. "Is this it?"

Tom took it from me and gave it a quick examination. "That's it. Where did you find it?"

"I found it in Jimmy's nightstand yesterday," I explained. "I couldn't figure out where it had come from. Did any of you ever see him wear it?"

None of us, other than Tom, knew anything about it or had ever seen Jimmy wear it, but we were all relieved to have its mysterious appearance explained.

I remembered the day that Jimmy and Tom had run the L.A. Marathon. When Jimmy and Evan turned twenty-three in 2006, they threw a party in Los Angeles. By a strange coincidence, Jimmy and Evan share the same birthday, a fact they didn't realize until they had used their fake IDs to get into a bar when they were nineteen. The bouncer looked at Evan's, then at Jimmy's. "You guys have the same birthday!" he exclaimed. It wasn't until they sat at the bar and compared their real drivers' licenses that they realized they actually had been born on the same day.

Tom had attended the birthday party. "I'm training with some of the Endeavor agents to run the Los Angeles Marathon in March. You interested, Jim?"

"It would be a great way to get back in shape," Jimmy mused. He also thought it couldn't hurt to get to know some of the top agents in the entertainment industry. "Yes, sir! I'm all in," he said.

Jimmy was always fast. In high school he was a wide receiver and ran track—sprints and high jump—but he was not a distance runner. I don't think he'd ever run a 10K. He'd also fallen out of shape over the last few years, claiming to be burned out from four years of high school football and year-round workouts. He also started smoking in college, just like his old man.

Jimmy really enjoyed the training and shared lots of stories about the runs they took, including a particularly wild jaunt on the Saturday before Thanksgiving. Tom, Jimmy, and two other Endeavor agents, Bill Weinstein and Rich Cook, were halfway into a fifteen-miler in the Malibu hills when Rich slipped on the trail. When the guys ran back to him, Rich was writhing in pain, his arm and shoulder at an odd angle.

The three tried to get Rich up on his feet, but the pain was excruciating. Tom took charge. "Jim, you stay here with Rich. Keep the mountain lions away. Bill and I will run to the ranger station and get help."

"But that's miles away!" Bill protested.

"Got any better ideas?" Tom said. Silence answered him. Then Bill began to jog back down the trail. Tom followed. Jimmy tried to make Rich comfortable, occasionally patting his head as you would a lapdog.

More than an hour later, the whump-whump-whump of a Los Angeles County Emergency Rescue helicopter reverberated through the hills. The chopper touched down in a clearing nearby, and two paramedics jumped out. In minutes, they had stabilized Rich's broken collarbone, put him on a stretcher, and loaded him in the helicopter. Jimmy jumped in and they were airlifted to the beach several miles away where Tom, Bill, and an ambulance were waiting.

There would be no marathon for Rich. However, the hard work paid off for the rest of the team and on March 4, 2007, Tom, Bill, and Jimmy successfully tackled the ordeal. Tom notched a personal best marathon time.

Jimmy wrote an e-mail about his run. Part of it said, "Finish line— Even though 2115 people had run across that line before I got there, the crowd was nice enough to make me feel like I'd won something. They cheered on repeat, which was very generous. A finisher's medal was put around my neck, but it felt so heavy I wanted to take it off. The thing must have weighed ten pounds at that moment.

"That night, marathon personal record setter Tom Strickler took us all out for Korean BBQ. The Kobe beef and cow tongue were savory. It was a great day. I recommend the marathon to everyone. Just Run."

That summed up Jimmy's life in two words. And if the premonition revealed in one of the most powerful things he ever wrote is true, he's still running.

At Jimmy's service, Evan read a poem Jimmy wrote shortly after completing the marathon. We had never seen or heard of it before. Tom gave us a copy of the poem when he visited. He has the original. Jimmy had given it to him as a thank you for "the push" to complete his first 26.2 miler, and for the Rolex. The title of the poem is "Suffering is the Only Honest Work," a testament to the grind of training and the battles between mind and body as the race with yourself extends into mile seventeen and beyond. But it was the last stanza that sent chills down our spines and filled us with wonder.

I.

Rich lay flat in the tall grass,
And you had a reason to run.
I'd stay with the writhing wounded,
Come help or a mountain lion.

Hope against panic, this was real,
A chance to make use of our bodies,
A chance to be men in the flesh.

And the joy in your step
As you bounded away
Took with it the shame of my joy.

We bonded in the fracture of a collarbone.

II.

Suffering is the only honest work,
Pain's wail the only song whose words
Can't be gargled in the cynic's throat,
Reduced to truth, then spat to the walls,
Bitter karaoke...

Thus, pain is irreducible, pain is true,
Suffering the only honest work.
False wisdom! You showed me otherwise,
On the run...

Mile seventeen-point-two...
I can't go on!
Seventeen-point-four...
My lips are cold, and the sun is warm.
Seventeen-five...
The wall, the wall, the fucking wall!
Seventeen-six...
No more! I can't! Not anymore!
(As six more steps plod the asphalt)
Interrogate the body!
Purge it of its false intelligence!

III.
That the flesh is deceitful
Is divine consolation,

And in periods of keenest pain
I'll know that I've run through walls,
That doubt is a bad idea,
And this death not even a trailhead
On the endless loop through ourselves;
That when my body lies flat in the tall grass,
The rest of me bounds up the hill.

Was this poem Jimmy's presentiment of a life about to be cut short? Were his words meant as reassurance for those of us he left so suddenly? That death is not an end?

Jimmy's body didn't make it past his twenty-fourth milestone, but he has never once stopped running up the hill—and he has taken great strides to let us all know that.

September 2008

One clear end-of-summer Sunday, Brittany and I drove up to Hollywood. We could no longer put off gathering Jimmy's things from his cabin in Laurel Canyon. The northbound I-5 freeway wasn't too crowded, and we made good time. James Taylor's song, "Sadie," from his recently released *Covers* album blasted from the CD player.

We didn't talk much on the drive up. I was lost in anxiety, dread, and the unknown of what the day would bring. Hilary didn't join us. The thought of being surrounded by all of our son's things—things he touched, wore, slept in—in the last place he had been before coming down for a visit those several Fridays ago, was just too hard for her. I also had the feeling that she wanted to put off the finality of Jimmy's death. As long as his belongings were still in his cabin, she could pretend that maybe he wasn't really gone.

It had taken Hilary and me weeks to finally read the latest draft of

Now's The Time. When Jimmy brought it to us, he said he'd been working furiously to finish it so he could show it to us before he took off on his trip to Vietnam. Jimmy never showed us rough or incomplete drafts. This version was so completely different from the one he had given us over a year earlier. Edgier. Darker. Not as innocent or sweet as before. The last two pages were typewritten notes, a very rough skeleton for the final scenes. He had not finished this version. He had run out of time, and deep down I think he knew it.

I looked over at my daughter. If you were to meet Brittany for the first time, you would no doubt be struck dumb by her stunning beauty. She is blessed with a physical attractiveness and presence that glows and shimmers and takes over any room she enters. And because of her extraordinary good looks, unless you began a conversation with her, you would not assume nor realize that she is one of the most intelligent, intuitive, and sensitive human beings on the planet, with an emotional IQ that is off the charts.

She has been one of the special ones since the day she was born— February 29, 1980. Since she was a little girl, Brittany has been surrounded by a large group of very close friends, girls and boys, men and women, who seek her out for counsel and advice on issues ranging from "Should I dump this boyfriend?" to "Should I go on living?" She is a confidante, and her friends have always entrusted her completely with their most personal feelings and revelations. She deeply cares about her friends and embraces their pain and heartaches and enhances their joys and exuberances. It was not chance that she majored in psychology at USC, spent two years working for Cancer Care in New York City, earned a master's degree in social work from San Diego State University and now works with a team of psychiatrists at the University of California at San Diego in the development and implementation of a program to prevent doctors and medical students from committing suicide.

Jimmy was her brother, of course, but Brittany, almost four years his senior, was also his closest friend. Sure, they fought and Brittany teased the daylights out of him when they were little, but as they grew older they adored and respected one another. Brittany always had Jimmy's back, and he would do anything to protect his big sister.

Brittany was completely and utterly blindsided by Jimmy's death. I never wanted my children to experience the kind of crushing pain and shock I'd felt when my father died. And I honestly believed they would never have to because I thought, to borrow a line from good friend and fraternity brother Ron Guss, I had already taken the "hit" for the family. My suffering, my pain, should satisfy whatever forces that governed our lives and leave my family happy forever.

Yet here we were, driving to Laurel Canyon to remove Jimmy's physical imprints on this place, and I was struck by our daughter's exceptional strength, courage, and toughness. I already knew these things about her. In 2001 she had suffered a major, full blackout, grand mal seizure that resulted in a car crash on the 405 freeway in West Los Angeles in which, miraculously, neither she nor anyone else was hurt, and over the past seven years had aggressively and proactively managed her health and lifestyle to live as normal and productive a life as possible with epilepsy.

As we floated northbound on Interstate 5, suddenly saucer-sized drops of clear liquid spattered the windshield. At least fifty of them hit simultaneously, obscuring all visibility. Blinded, I hit the windshield wipers.

"What the heck was that?" Brittany screamed, her eyes wide with alarm.

"Bugs?" I suggested, even though there was no yellowish-brown sticky film, wings, parts, or yucky residue typical of bug splat. We glanced at the twenty or so cars surrounding us. None of them had their wipers going. They appeared utterly unaffected by whatever slammed into our windshield.

"I think we've just been slimed," Brittany said, referring to the gooey mess the ghosts left when sliding through people and walls in *Ghostbusters*.

An eerie feeling, not evil or bad, just strange, came over me. Maybe this was Jimmy's way of letting us know he was still around and he would help with the mission looming ahead of us. The feeling was so strong that I glanced over my shoulder to see if he—or anyone—might be sitting in the backseat.

By the time we got to Jimmy's place on Lookout Mountain Road, we had concluded that something very unusual had happened and couldn't wait to tell Evan and John Dale, another close friend of Jimmy's, about it.

They were already there when we arrived, just as they've always been there. Hugs and subdued words of greeting. Then we walked single file up the rather tipsy path to the cabin. I unlocked the door and we went in.

Whenever I visited I felt like Gulliver trying to live in a Lilliputian house. Yet the place suited Jimmy, cool and kind of bohemian. In the late sixties, Joni Mitchell and David Crosby had partied and written music in a house near this cabin. Sometimes a faint echo of her song, "Lady of the Canyon," seemed to drift on the breeze. Jimmy fit in here.

The place was just as Jimmy had left it the Friday he'd come home. Sun streamed through the uncurtained windows, lighting up the room. An empty Rolex Explorer box was on Jimmy's writing desk. "Well, where do we start?" I asked.

John walked over and turned on the stereo. "Might as well have some music while we work," he said as he slipped a vinyl LP out of its cover. The Brazilian rhythms of Juan Carlos Jobim filled the room as I handed out plastic garbage sacks. Interesting selection. My father was a huge Jobim fan.

"Let's collect his clothes and we'll donate them to that homeless shelter down on Sunset," Evan suggested.

John headed for the closet. "Oh, man, look at these," he said, holding up a pair of corduroy pants that were obviously too short for Jimmy. "That guy didn't care what he wore." He rummaged farther and found balls of Banana Republic T-shirts of brown, olive green, and beige hues tossed in a mildewed corner of the closet. "Man, I remember when he bought this from Goodwill," he said holding up a well-worn brown leather bomber jacket from Nordstrom, which I'd not seen before.

And of course, there were the books. Evan shook his head, smiling. "I swear to God, Jimmy would read anything that didn't walk away." Brittany laughed as she filled a cardboard box with well-thumbed volumes.

As we packed and bagged, we took turns playing random selections from Jimmy's considerable collection of vinyl on the turntable I had given to him the year before: Charlie Parker, Miles Davis, Stan Getz. Occasionally we heard the muffled sounds of voices and live music reverberating off the canyon walls, sounds of life going on around us, life lived by people we would never know and who would never know of us or our impossible task. For a moment, I imagined sitting on Jimmy's porch perched on the hillside late on a summer evening and listening to Joni Mitchell and David Crosby rehearsing "The Dawntreader" a few doors up the steep, narrow road.

My heart lifted. Instead of a dreadful, tear-filled farewell, this day had turned into a tender memorial to an amazing man whom I'd been proud to call my son. Each of us staked claim to at least one of his belongings. John requested the turntable and records, Brittany had already asked for his writing table, and Evan took the well-used espresso machine. I went home with the leather jacket and the empty Rolex box.

As we made our way down the path, I glanced back. For a split second, I imagined Jimmy lounging on the porch, a smile, lifting a hand in farewell.

ITASCA

I WAS BORN AT Seaside Hospital in Long Beach, California, on January 13, 1950. Friday the thirteenth. My folks named me Vernon Case Gauntt, after my maternal grandfather, but I've always gone by Casey. I am a fifth-generation Californian and a seventh-generation American on my mother's side and eleventh-generation American on my father's side.

We lived in the Naples area of Long Beach, and at the time my father was working for his father-in-law's company, Case Foundation Company. Vern Case had become interested in the foundation drilling business and thought the Midwest would be a hotbed for work. In early 1951 he asked my dad to set up an office near Detroit. He and his wife Henrietta would remain in Los Angeles.

My father travelled a lot, hustling and supervising construction work, and he was becoming dissatisfied with a lot of things, including working for Vern. He reluctantly decided to leave Case Foundation and in January of 1953 we moved back to Los Angeles, where he got a job with Anthony Swimming Pools. We settled into the recently completed Park La Brea Towers apartments near the corner of Fairfax and Third. My dad may have left Case, but he didn't get very far from the Cases. Vern and Henrietta were living in one of the penthouse apartments at Park La Brea.

My dad decided to partner with a co-worker at Anthony Pools and build homes. They bought some orange grove land in West Covina and started building houses. In 1954 we moved into one of them. It even had a pool!

However, my father's decision came at the wrong time. The Veterans Administration cracked down on housing loans for vets, leaving him and his partner land poor, with several unsold houses. By this time Vern and Henrietta had moved to Keeneyville, a suburb of Chicago, and set up the new headquarters for Case Foundation.

In October of 1955 Dad wrote a letter to his mother-in-law. She talked to Vern, and he was rehired. We moved into a house on Greenview Road in Itasca in February 1956, the same month Elvis' new song, "Heartbreak Hotel," was released. Prophetic? My mom may have been happy to be near her folks, but for my dad, going back to work for Case Foundation was a painful reminder that he couldn't make it on his own. This would have serious repercussions, though not for many years.

Vern was not an easy man to work for, and my father knew only too well what he was getting back into. Vern paid off his debts, bought the house for us in Itasca, and gave him a job, all generous gestures, but with the sternly delivered condition, "Don't you ever quit on me again!" The psychological strings may have been invisible, but they were unbreakable. My father was now, financially and emotionally, even more deeply indebted to his father-in-law.

Itasca was the quintessential Midwest town, quiet, reserved, surrounded by farms and linked to Chicago by the Milwaukee Railroad. Our town was so small that the main drag, Irving Park Road, which paralleled the railroad tracks, didn't have a stop sign or a traffic light. Cars and trucks just blew through town at high speed.

Across the highway The Lampliter catered to the cocktail crowd, while Ed's Standard Oil gassed and greased cars. The police station and the volunteer fire department sat next to each other. Between the highway and the fire and police stations was a pond that froze in the winter, making the perfect ice hockey rink.

The Lutheran church, with its prominent white steeple, and the water tower with "ITASCA" painted in bold black letters, were the town landmarks. Our Presbyterian church perched on a high hill just outside the town center. Whenever I went to town, I had to hike or bike up that hill. The return trip was great, though. Without pedaling, I could coast about a quarter of mile down Center Street along the ninth and tenth holes of the Itasca Country Club golf course.

Walnut Street was the center of what passed for the business district. Shumann's Bakery, the Itasca State Bank, a pharmacy, and the phone company building were prominent. The Itasca Basket supplied the grocery needs of the town. Dr. Bowman saw to our medical needs.

Whenever I had a dime for a comic book, I'd head for The News Agency, which sold newspapers, magazines, model kits, squirt guns, and kites. But my favorite store was Matt's, a tiny grocery next to the railroad tracks. The building was in such poor shape that it constantly threatened to fall down around anyone who happened to be inside when a train rumbled past. The danger involved in entering that sacred place only heightened my excitement. Snaps, Lik-M-Ade, Jujubes, jawbreakers, Charleston Chews, and all the other candy so dear to a growing boy's heart filled one long shelf, and I would spend hours, and most of my allowance, choosing my favorites.

North School housed kindergarten through eighth grade, and the kids from Washington Elementary, which opened in 1960 on the other side of town, came to North for junior high.

There wasn't much to do in Itasca. With only two channels available on our small black-and-white television, sitting around the house didn't hold much appeal, either. Our moms drove us ten miles if we wanted to see a movie or go bowling. Our house backed onto the eleventh hole of the golf course, a blessing when at six I discovered how much fun golf was. I spent half my life on the links until I graduated from high school and went to work in West Virginia.

When my hair needed cutting or I wanted a library book or just wanted to go to town to see what was happening, I'd jump on my cherry red Schwinn bike that I'd tricked out with baseball cards clipped on the fenders so they'd slap against the spokes of the rear wheels, making a whizzing sound as I rode. In the interests of being cool, I had also turned the handlebars upside down. I was sure that everyone I zipped past was admiring my ride, and I sat tall in the saddle, hands raised above my head, proud to own such a marvelous machine.

For such a small town, it was a bit of a mystery how Itasca could support two barber shops. Mr. Lund and Jerry had been partners, but they had a fight and Jerry started his own shop, which was sandwiched between the library and The News Agency. Mr. Lund's shop flanked Schumann's Bakery. I considered Lund's to be the clear winner in the location battle, but in order to be fair and keep the peace, we split our business between the shops. I thought a haircut every two weeks was excessive, but my mom insisted. Keeping our flattops short and neat was one of the rules of our home.

My brother G.G. was nearly three years older and wouldn't be caught dead going to the barber at the same time as me, and that was just fine. In some ways, I wished we could be as close as the characters in my favorite TV shows—Wally and Beaver, or Ricky and David Nelson—but he preferred that I keep out of his business, and I mostly did, unless I was looking for a fight.

I longed for the day when Mr. Lund would shave my sideburns and neck. I couldn't just ask him to perform that most important rite of passage, however. He decided when a boy was man enough to undergo the ritual of hot lather and straight razor. I was fourteen and had not yet reached puberty when Mr. Lund reached for the shaving cup. I closed my eyes as the handle of the brush clinked against the cup. The soap scent engulfed my nostrils as the sable bristles caressed my temples, nape, and sideburns. When the razor touched my skin, I knew I had attained barbershop manhood.

When it snowed or rained, I walked the mile into town and back to get my hair cut. My mother would not drive me unless the temperature was below zero, claiming that the exercise was good for me. On frigid days, I swore that a fiend had stolen her soul and was forcing her to torture me. When I considered the proximity of Schumann's Bakery to Mr. Lund's, the fairness doctrine of splitting our business equally between the two barber shops spiraled away on the howling wind. A twist donut and a cup of hot chocolate fortified me for the death march home.

With the luxury of hindsight, I realize that, in spite of my childhood perception of nothing to do, we kids owned the town. Unless we were grounded, we could go anywhere, any time, and play for hours. A casual shout of "'Bye, Mom!" and her return shout of "Be back for dinner!" were enough to free me to seek adventure on my tricked-out bike. In good weather, my friends and I would play baseball, football, basketball, and field hockey, using tennis balls for pucks. Sometimes we'd head for North School and smack the tetherball around its pole or play wall ball, our version of dodge ball, against the three-story solid brick wall in back of the building.

Even though our bikes were our most treasured possessions, bike tag enticed us into a scaled-down version of demolition derby. We raced our bikes around, charging at other boys, slamming on the brakes to skid into them without doing too much damage to our own. When we made contact with another kid's pride and joy, he was out.

After dinner, we'd gather in the dusk for nightly games of kick the can, red rover, and pompom pull-away. Or we'd hide in the shadows and tell ghost stories and tall tales of what we wanted to be when we grew up. Pro golfers, major league pitchers, race car drivers, spies, President: Who knew such a small town could house so much ambition?

When the town lay blanketed in Midwestern winter, we hauled tobog-gans and skis to the steepest hills on the golf course. When rain froze, the streets became our rink, and we'd skate for blocks, safe because most drivers wouldn't venture out on the slick streets. Spring thaws flooded low-lying areas of the golf course; our homemade rafts became the vessels on which we ruled the mighty waterways. When the winds blew strong in the spring and fall, we'd "borrow" bed sheets, launching ourselves off the same hills we'd tobogganed down, hoping to soar to altitude, always disappointed. Two creeks wound through town, and every kid had a fishing pole.

We had plenty to do, and we were free. Crime, other than an occasional speeding driver, was unknown to us. Our parents never worried about us as long as we were careful crossing Irving Park Road. Which I usually was, until one strange event happened.

Late one summer afternoon I was biking across town to Washington

Park for a Little League game. When I got to Irving, I dismounted and began to walk across the road. The next thing I remember was being on the opposite side of the road, facing traffic, and everything was moving in slow motion. A red-and-white station wagon was only a few yards past the point where I was standing and holding my bike. Its blaring horn was an arrow of sound shooting through my eardrums. The driver thrust a hairy arm out his window and shook his fist. "You wanna get yourself killed?"

When I started across the road, I never saw that car or any other coming. For the life of me, I don't know how I made it across without getting hit. I got back on my bike and rode a block or so. Then I began shaking and sobbing. I got off, sat down on the sidewalk, and cried for a long time, wondering what in the heck had just happened.

Other kids in town weren't so lucky. In 1959, a boy named Peterson who was a couple of years older than my brother collapsed and died as he ran home from football practice. Robbie Robuck, a year older than I, and his younger sister were playing with matches in their basement one afternoon in 1963. Her dress caught on fire and before Robbie could chase her down and put out the flames, she burned to death. That same year my seventh-grade classmate, Karen, who lived a few houses away, died of leukemia.

My friend Buddy Wheaton dodged death because of a phone call. One February night in 1967, a blizzard had buried the entire Chicago area in snow. Two of Buddy's friends, Rodney Hendrickson and Gary Olsen, planned to hitch a toboggan to the rear bumper of a car belonging to one of their classmates and ride across Roselle, a town that neighbored Itasca. Buddy thought that would be a fine adventure and agreed to go with them.

As Buddy waited in his driveway for them to pick him up, his mother yelled out the door, "Buddy! You have a phone call."

"Tell 'em I'll call when I get back," he replied.

"It's Kathy," Mrs. Wheaton said. Buddy's girlfriend had missed several days of school due to illness, so Buddy went inside and took the call.

"Hi, Buddy," Kathy said. "Can you bring your biology book over? I want to catch up on my homework."

"Sure. Be right there," he replied.

As he backed the family car down the driveway, Rodney and Gary pulled up. "You coming with?" Rodney asked.

"Can't," Buddy replied, holding up his textbook. "Kathy wants to catch up on her homework. Have fun."

They drove off, intent on their upcoming thrill ride. They never returned. As the tow car flew across an intersection, another car sped through. It missed the car but smashed into the toboggan. Rodney and Gary were killed instantly.

MY FATHER

My thought process has been prejudiced by a depression in my youth and insecurity, by a religious fanatical mother who I could not reason with, by a war in which I was in the infantry, and so forth.

Grover C. Gauntt, Jr., June 19, 1968

THOUGH LIFE SEEMS to be lived linearly, we gather information sporadically, sometimes not becoming privy to relevant knowledge until well after events that seem inexplicable when they happen. If I had known more about my father's past, I might have been less appalled and more empathetic when he died. As it was, I discovered far too late the influences that shaped the man who meant more to me than anyone except Jimmy.

Grover Cleveland Gauntt, Jr., was born in 1919 in Fort Worth, Texas, and named after his father, who went by the nickname "Bud." Bud, the only son of John Randolph Gauntt and Nannie Zelda Curtis, was born in 1888 in New York, Texas, ten miles east of Athens and about a hundred miles southeast of Fort Worth. Bud got a kick out of telling people he was born in New York and lived in Athens.

When Bud was sixteen he moved to Fort Worth and found work at a department store that featured women's ready-to-wear clothing. Nine years later, he married Frances Imogene Brooks. Their two oldest daughters, Imogene and Mary Jane, were born in Fort Worth. In 1923 Bud moved the family to Oklahoma City, where he became a partner in another women's clothing store. When the establishment went bust a year later, the family packed up and moved to Glendale, California. Bud got a job with Webb's Department Store, again selling women's apparel. Their youngest and last child, Anna Louise, came along in 1925.

Bud and Frances followed the teachings and practices of Mary Baker Eddy, the founder of Christian Science, relying on prayer and mental treatment to heal physical maladies. Diphtheria, a highly contagious infection of the upper respiratory system, had never heard of Mrs. Eddy and her philosophy, and in 1933, it struck the family hard. Imogene's and Anna's throats became coated in a thick, gray membrane as they complained of sore throats and swollen glands. Fever set them trembling as their breathing became labored and shallow. Barking coughs echoed through the house as their parents prayed.

My father, only fourteen, watched helplessly as eight-year-old Anna succumbed to the deadly disease in spite of the fact that a vaccine was now available that could have saved her. Two days later Bud wrapped Imogene in blankets and drove her to the hospital, where doctors administered the vaccine. Imogene eventually recovered.

Grover Jr. was extremely close to and protective of his little sister and could never understand why his folks didn't save her. Bud had lost his youngest sister to the same disease when she was four years old. How in God's name could he have let his own daughter die?

After Anna's death, their mother, Frances, became obsessed with a religion that had something to do with the Twelve Tribes of Israel. Every Friday evening and Saturday and Sunday mornings, Bud drove her to Inglewood, twenty miles away, where she spent all day in church.

Frances had kept her figure in spite of having borne four children, and her features were fine and lovely. Her children took after her. Now she gave up wearing makeup and dressed plainly. Apparently because of her religious beliefs, she removed all family photographs and pictures from the house. Grover Jr. and his sisters cringed each time she took up her tracts and marched around the neighborhood, knocking on doors and preaching to those bold enough to answer.

As she became more deeply involved in her new religion, some came to believe that she was a medium with the ability to communicate with those who had passed over. Others put her strange ways down to mental illness. "She's not all there," folks said, and her son agreed.

Bud traveled more on business, taking several trips each year to the "other" New York City to buy the latest women's fashions for his store. With Frances becoming more and more immersed in her proselytizing, Imogene had to take over much of the role of mother to Mary Jane and Grover Jr. The family was slowly torn apart.

Mary Jane attended Glendale High School, where her beauty and brains gained her a following. She was immensely popular, a cheerleader, and a class officer. Imogene had enrolled at UCLA, where she became the school's first homecoming queen. Perhaps these two gorgeous girls were the reason why so many of the upper classmen at Glendale High and UCLA befriended my dad.

However, he didn't have to piggyback on his sisters for his popularity. He consistently made the honor roll, boxed, played decent football, and was student body president of both his junior high and high school. He was also a very good-looking guy. I guess it must be in the genes.

In 1937, money was tight. Bud handed his son twenty-seven dollars to cover the first couple of quarters of tuition at UCLA. After that, he was on his own. He joined the Phi Kappa Psi fraternity and majored in geology. He worked all through college at a men's clothing store near campus and also delivered corsages to sorority girls for extra cash. I once asked my mother if he had ever worked in his father's store in Glendale and she said, "Your father rarely set foot in that store. He did not respect his father and his line of work."

He joined the Army Reserve Officers Training Corps (ROTC) as a junior. Even though America was not yet in the war against the Germans and Japanese, everyone thought it was only a matter of time before we were dragged in, and when that day came he wanted to go in as an officer.

In the spring of his junior year, a fraternity brother, Frank Gehri, woke him up late one Saturday night and shouted "G.G., get up! I went out with this great gal tonight. She's downstairs in my car and I want to introduce you to her. She's a Pi Phi and a freshman at USC."

Groggy and grumpy, he threw on his robe and followed his slightly inebriated pal downstairs. As he approached Frank's car, a long-legged, impeccably dressed, gorgeous redhead unfolded herself from the front seat and emerged onto the sidewalk.

Frank said, "Grover, I'd like you to meet Barbara Case."

My mother loved to tell the story of that first meeting. "I was a little flustered. There was something about him. I told a joke and he didn't laugh. He just looked at me with no expression. I was embarrassed and figured, well, he must not think too much of me." Shows how wrong one can be.

A few weeks later, Gehri took Barbara to a dinner club in Santa Monica. Grover and a date were at a nearby table. Barbara recalled, "At some point in the evening I looked over to your dad's table. He smiled at me and let a pea fall out of his mouth. He called me up a few days later and that's how the whole thing started."

Peas were his shtick. When we were kids, if he was in a rare comedic mood during dinner, a pea would drop out of his mouth or, better, his nose. My sister, Laura, would double over with laughter. My mother found it less amusing.

Immediately upon graduation in 1941 my father went into the Army as a second lieutenant. His first posting was Fort Ord on beautiful Monterey Bay, a hundred miles south of San Francisco. Then he went to Camp Roberts near San Luis Obispo, a two-hour drive south. The Japanese Imperial Navy attacked Pearl Harbor December 7, 1941. The United States immediately declared war on Japan and Germany and the training became intense.

Barbara had not seen or heard from Grover for over six months since he joined the Army, but she learned from his sister, Mary Jane, that the Gauntt family was planning to be in Willits for Christmas. Vern Case had grown up in Willits in northern California and had a bunch of family there. Barbara begged her father to drive from their home in West Los Angeles to Willits for the holidays. Barbara and Grover "bumped in" to one another, and my mother said it was "Love at first re-sight." They would be together until his death.

Grover Jr. was promoted to the rank of Captain and commander of the Cannon Company of the 145th Infantry Division in April of 1943, and his unit continued to train in San Luis Obispo. By this time, almost all of his fraternity brothers and good friends had joined up and were spread across the four corners of the world. They tried to stay in touch, but it was very difficult. In his letters to Barbara and his folks he would often ask if there was any word about a particular friend or friends. He specifically asked of his good friend, Jim Simmons, who had been sent to the Aleutian Islands off the coast of Alaska with the 17th Infantry Division, the one my father was originally assigned to. He had heard rumors that the Army underreported the number of U.S. soldiers killed on Attu, one of the islands. He found out a month later his pal Jim was one of them.

In his letters to Barbara there was more than worry of the unknown. There was love—head-over-heels, puppy-dog love. In January of 1943 he wrote, "I want to see you more than ever before. Just seeing you for such a short time my last trip home made something pop. You are the only one." And one month later, "I'm thinking of you constantly, in fact believe me, you get in my way mentally. I often catch myself not working—my mind is playing with you."

They were young, and their longing for each other was urgent. There was nothing more important and present for them than that very next moment they would be together. Their romance was mostly long distance—letters and an occasional phone call, when one could get through.

Grover's intense training kept him on base, while Barbara finished at USC. Then she made a decision that thrust them even farther apart. When she graduated in 1943, she joined the Women's Army Auxiliary Corps. The WACs were assigned to the multitude of jobs that didn't involve firing a gun: recruiting, office work, switchboard, and mechanical duties. Every job filled by a WAC equaled one more man who could be sent to the front lines.

All well and good, except for the fact she neglected to discuss this in advance with Captain Gauntt, and he was not happy. Pissed is more like it. After basic training in Arkansas, Second Lieutenant Barbara Case was ordered to Iowa on a recruiting detail. With over half a continent between them, they had no chance of seeing one another.

Even worse was the possibility of her being shipped overseas to a danger zone. Teletype operators, lab technicians, mail sorters, and rifle and truck repair women weren't guaranteed a safe berth in the States. Figuratively biting his tongue to keep from lambasting her, he wrote, "I'm taken by surprise. I hope you will be satisfied. I do hope, Barbara, that you will be happy, and that you find all of your expectations."

Barbara was exhibiting the strength and independence she inherited from her parents, Henrietta and Vern. She defiantly told me many years later, "Look, your dad was going to be shipped out any day. I was not going to wait around in my parents' house and sit on my hands with nothing else to do but worry about him and whether he was going to come home. I needed to do something. I needed to get involved, too."

The 145th received orders to ship out in December 1943. Grover and Barbara made it home to Los Angeles and spent Christmas with their families and each other. A couple of days later, Barbara drove him to Camp Roberts. The serenity of this side of the Pacific Ocean as they drove north belied the conflict raging thousands of miles to the west. She drove alone back to Los Angeles, listening to Ma Perkins and stories of the war on the radio, tears streaming down her cheeks most of the way. Captain Gauntt and his men boarded ships in San Francisco on December 30th, their destination the Solomon Islands in the South Pacific, aka Hell.

The 145th landed on Bougainville in February 1944, where the Solomon Sea meets the South Pacific. As World War II broke out, the Japanese had seized the Solomon Islands as well as most of Southeast Asia. The U.S. planned to move north, up through the Solomons, clearing out Japanese defense and air support along the way, and then attack the Philippines and finally Japan. In 1942 the Marines wiped the Japanese out of the first Solomon Island, Guadalcanal, and in 1943 the Army's 37th Infantry Division captured New Georgia.

Bougainville was the last Japanese stronghold in the Solomons. The 3rd Marine Division and the Army's 37th invaded Bougainville in November

1943, landing at Empress Augusta Bay. They took control of six of the two hundred fifty square miles comprising this island and built an airbase to provide security and supplies for the convoys that would be assembled to retake the Philippines. Pushing across the island to take on the 25,000 Japanese dug in the mountainous jungles wasn't in the plan.

The Japanese eventually realized the Americans weren't coming for them and, if they wanted to take out the Americans' newly installed airfield, they would have to bring the fight to them. The perimeter of the U.S. base was surrounded by thick jungle, laced with rivers and dominated by a towering land mass rising above it all known as Hill 700. The 145th Infantry Division's first combat assignment was to defend Hill 700. The Japanese began their assault shortly after midnight on March 8, 1944. Sargent John McLeod described the ensuing battle for *Yank Magazine*.

"It was just a wet, cold, muddy jungle with everything bad about it that could be bad. It was air raids that sent you from hammock or cot into a slit trench five or six times a night. It was the constant rumble of guns. It was myriads of snapping ants and mosquitoes and centipedes whose sting was so bad they made a litter case out of more than one man. For the line companies it was all that and worse. It was patrols over mountains and icy rivers and dripping jungles. It was being constantly drenched by rain, rivers and sweat. At night it was sleeping in water-filled slit trenches with a shelter half around your head to discourage the mosquitoes. It was also getting over the fear complexes. It was learning that the Japanese were not so hot after all. It was learning that the Jap soldier is, as often as not, cocky and foolish and will walk into an ambush. It was sitting behind your own perimeter and letting the Japs come up and then blasting hell out of them all night. It was counting over 1,000 Japanese dead in half the concentration area the next morning." [*Yank Magazine*, Sgt. John McLeod, August 1945]

During the 145th's baptism to combat, 5,500 Japanese soldiers were killed and over 3,000 wounded. Captain Gauntt received his first Bronze Star for heroism exhibited during the fierce battle. He was twenty-four. A couple of weeks later he wrote his folks: "I'm beginning to become restless and dream of pushing on. I have a fancy for fighting that you would never be able to comprehend or I explain. Maybe I will get my fill too soon. By the way, I had returned today a letter I wrote to Gehri. There's another one gone." The fraternity brother who introduced him to Barbara had been shot down and killed somewhere over the Philippines.

Before leaving Bougainville, my father was promoted to Major, making him the youngest Army officer in the Pacific Theater to achieve that rank. The 145th shipped out in December 1944 and made their way to Luzon, the largest of the thousands of islands making up the Philippines and home to its capital and largest city, Manila. Upon landing in the Lingayen Gulf, they made a hundred-sixty-mile run for Manila through the Luzon Valley. It truly was a "run," with the troops slogging up to thirty-plus miles a day through dense jungle, fish ponds, rice paddies, and flooded rivers. On the way they inflicted heavy casualties on the Japanese. On February 3, the 145th arrived at the doorstep of Manila.

Twenty thousand Japanese troops were embedded in the city. Every building, down to the crypts at the cemeteries, had been converted into fortified bunkers manned with heavily armed Japanese soldiers. After twenty days of U.S. forces advancing building by building, crypt by crypt, in brutal hand-to-hand fighting, Manila was turned into a rubble pile. Over 4,000 Japanese were killed, thousands more wounded, and the rest either captured or routed out of the city and into the surrounding countryside. American casualties were equally staggering. Forty percent of the men of the 145th were killed or otherwise rendered unable to fight. Many thought the Division was washed up. A few weeks later the remaining units of the 145th were attached to the Army's 6th Division and sent to Mount Pacawagan, fourteen miles east of Manila.

Pacawagan was the most dominant of the three mountains in this region, each over 1,500 feet of steep slopes, precipitous canyons, and sheer vertical peaks. Pacawagan was riddled with a maze of bunkers, caves, tunnels, and trenches occupied by several thousand soldiers of the Japanese elite Shimbu Line armed with one of the heaviest concentrations of enemy artillery in the entire Philippines. Sgt. Frank J. Ward of the 145th told *Yank Magazine* that Mt. Pacawagan was worse than New Georgia, Bougainville, and Manila combined. "You never heard of Mt. Pacawagan, did you? I guess no one has. While we were up there, the war in Europe ended. I imagine people at home were too busy celebrating that to read about places with names like Mt. Pacawagan."

The battle for Mt. Pacawagan began on April 21, 1945, under cover of darkness. A daylight approach would have made the U.S. soldiers as vulnerable as ducks on a pond, given the enemy's superior firing positions and the difficult terrain. The troops assembled at the base of the mountain and at 4:00 a.m. the 145th launched an intense artillery barrage on the mountain. Lit only by the light of exploding shells, the men began the arduous climb up the mountain, groping hand-over-hand up slopes approaching 60 degrees, grasping the leg of the man ahead to maintain contact and prevent them from sliding down the mountain.

As dawn broke, the enemy rained a withering array of machine gun, artillery, and mortar fire down upon the advancing 145th. Enemy fire erupted from the caves, bunkers, pillboxes, and gullies embedded in the mountainsides. Fighting was hand to hand, and the Americans routed the enemy out of their positions with rifle fire, grenades, pole charges, flame throwers, and mortars. Progress was measured in feet; death was measured in thousands.

Four days into the battle, 2,000 American soldiers were now spread over the mountain and resupplying them with ammo, food, and water became paramount to their survival. As recounted by 145th Division Commander Colonel Loren Windom, "One event of tremendous importance occurred on April 25—the bulldozer supply trail was, after heartbreaking reverses, pushed to the top of Mt. Pacawagan." This enabled the troops to be resupplied and artillery to be dragged by tractors up the steep terrain to prepare for an attack. The next morning, the U.S. troops launched their assault and after bitter fighting, captured most of the mountain. Colonel Windom described the attack in his journal. "It was as if Mt. Pacawagan itself had suddenly turned into a huge volcano and erupted with a series of explosions. The sky was brilliant with myriad of fingers of tracer bullets of all calibers, the blinding flashes of heavy shells and the spectacular display of flying white phosphorous. The din of battle was deafening. Identification of friend and foe was nearly impossible in the darkness."

Major Gauntt was in charge of the construction of this supply-survival trail and he was awarded the Army's prestigious Legion of Merit and his second Bronze Star. In recommending him for this honor, Colonel Windom wrote, "As the troops advanced up the mountain, Major Gauntt repeatedly made personal reconnaissance for the extension of the road, and in so doing was often exposed to enemy rifle, machine gun, and mortar fire. When the troops reached the peak of the mountain, Major Gauntt had his supply road ready behind them. At the same time Major Gauntt organized a group of 600 civilian laborers for carrying supplies to the front line units. While two truckloads of natives were moving toward the supply point, several rounds of Japanese 75 mm artillery landed in the area, one round ten yards from one of the vehicles, instantly killing two and seriously wounding fourteen. Quickly administering all possible aid and still under artillery fire, Major Gauntt reorganized the panic-stricken natives and successfully led them to their destination. Major Grover C. Gauntt contributed immeasurably to the success with which the 145th Infantry operated."

Twenty-five days after commencing its attack, the 145th captured Mt. Pacawagan. The 145th suffered more than 700 casualties; over three times that number of men had to be evacuated from the front lines either permanently or temporarily for noncombat injuries, sickness, and psychoneurotic causes.

On August 6, the first atomic bomb, "Little Boy," decimated Hiroshima, Japan. Three days later "Fat Man" demolished Nagasaki. The Japanese surrendered on August 15, 1945, and World War II was over. By this time Major Gauntt had been promoted to Battalion Commander, one of the highest ranking officers in the 145th Division.

Historians estimate the 145th killed over 7,400 and captured 500 of the enemy on Luzon. Three hundred officers and enlisted men of the 145th were killed and more than 1,400 were wounded. Well over half of the men from the 145th who landed on Luzon were killed or wounded.

After the war ended, my father and what remained of the 145th were stuck on Luzon for another four months. He and his men were bored and eager to get home. He contracted malaria, another gift from the islands, and something else to fight while he awaited orders to ship home. He wrote Barbara on November 1, 1945, "Still at Camp La Croix and will be here another two weeks. There isn't anything to do, and I'll be damned if I'll go out of my way. I spend most of my time hoping that I'll be home for Xmas. I miss you darling, and want to see you—month is a long time—keep your fingers crossed."

Major Gauntt arrived at Long Beach harbor on December 13, 1945, two weeks shy of two years from when he left. My mother had been discharged from the WACs a month earlier and was staying with her folks in Coronado across the bay from San Diego. When she got word that my father would be landing, Barbara and her mother booked into a motel in West Los Angeles. There wouldn't be a scene of hugs and kisses at the dock as the men disembarked. Visitors weren't allowed at the port. They finally reunited at the motel and stayed out most of the night sitting in Henrietta's car talking and, well, getting reacquainted. Barbara remembers the next day Henrietta was furious with her for keeping Grover awake most of the night when he was exhausted and still recuperating from malaria. My mother recalls not feeling too bad about it. Two weeks later, over Christmas, Grover proposed to his best girl and they were married in Los Angeles on March 5, 1946. They were getting on with their lives.

ONE SUITCASE

L OSING JIMMY WASN'T my first foray into tragedy. My father died in 1970, three days before Christmas. I was twenty. My mother charged ahead, getting on with life. In fact, within three weeks after my dad's passing, she moved my thirteen-year-old sister, Laura, and herself from Itasca to Springville, California, to live with her folks while my brother, Grover, and I returned to college, me to USC and him to Wharton to finish his MBA. I sometimes wondered why she couldn't have done something, said something, that might have changed the outcome of that awful holiday, but then maybe she took care of herself the same way I had, stuffing emotions safely inside, never feeling the need to take them out, dust them off, and relive the pain.

Soon after Jimmy died she tried to take the same "We're going to move on with life and not talk about it" approach. I knew she thought she was helping me. *Run from the pain. Don't look back. Don't let it catch you. You got away before. Your dad didn't take you down.*

But I was tired of running and hiding. "Mom, it's time we stop, turn around, and look this thing in the eye. This time we're going to talk about it." And we did. We finally did.

Just before 2011 rolled into 2012, my mom fell, breaking her arm and her clavicle, which sent her to the hospital. Then pneumonia, COPD, and congestive heart failure made their appearances, which didn't surprise any of us, given her lifelong pack-a-day habit. The doctors had drawn more blood than her frail body could produce, or so it seemed. She cycled through skilled nursing and assisted living, and on this February evening finally was back in her own home. We didn't know then that it would be for only this one night. By morning, she would be back in the ER, fighting for breath. She would not return home; from today on, she would be cared for by doctors and nurses and those wonderful angels from hospice involved with the finalities of life. But for tonight, at least, she was ours.

Laura had flown from Switzerland to pitch in and help Hilary and me take care of her. The three of us sat in the living room of her house in High Country Villas, a seniors-only community in Encinitas, a few miles from our home. Her living room overlooked the fifth hole of the executive golf course. She loved the place, tolerated the parade of golfers passing by and the occasional errant tee shot landing on her patio.

As the day drifted into twilight and a straggle of golfers headed for the clubhouse, my mother sagged in a chair in the living room, tethered to the ubiquitous oxygen tank at her side. The chair's faded "wings" seemed to surround her, like those of a bird or perhaps an angel. I sat in its twin, my back and shoulders pressed defiantly into its bulk. Laura and Hilary were perched on dining chairs.

Even as her fragility seemed to increase by the moment, she seemed more alive, alert, and focused than I could ever remember her being, even as a young woman. Perhaps coming face-to-face with her mortality prompted her to talk about my dad, his death, and its brutal aftermath. "I'm so glad and grateful that you—" nodding toward Laura—"and Grover and Casey survived those days and weeks and months. I'm also thankful that you all seem to have come through it relatively sane. You know, I never hesitated when people asked how Grover Jr. died. I came right out and told them. I didn't want people talking behind my back, wondering what really happened."

My heart hammered in my chest. *We were really going to talk about this.* As the conversation swirled around me, I heard many things I hadn't heard before. Each new piece of information inserted itself into a movie that began to play in my mind, a film noir I had put back in its canister decades earlier and shoved onto the farthest back shelf of my mind.

—⁀⁀—

December 1970. Dad, Mom, and Laura go to a movie, *Patton,* starring George C. Scott. An hour into the movie, he walks out. Too much war, too many memories. Battles he fought long ago in the South Pacific seem as if they were yesterday. He waits in the lobby and his wife and daughter join him a few minutes later.

They drive home, and Mom follows Dad into their bedroom. The door closes. Laura, distressed yet not knowing why, kneels with her ear to the keyhole. Soft murmuring is all she hears at first.

Then my dad says, "I just want to get in the car by myself and drive it into a tree."

My mother tosses him a lifeline. "Let's pack one suitcase and go. Anywhere you want. Let's just go, you and me, right now. Let's get away from all this."

Laura fights back tears as the voices quiet again. She hurries to her room. What will happen to her if her parents leave? She brushes away tears. No, they'd never leave her, especially Daddy. She's his princess. By the next morning the conversation has faded from her thirteen-year-old mind.

A few days later, she's lying on her bed, listening to Michael Jackson croon The Jackson 5's new release, "I'll Be There," over and over on the 45 record on her portable hi-fi. Dad comes to the door and looks at her for a long moment. Then he speaks. "You know I'll always love you, don't you?"

"Of course I do, Daddy," she replies, smiling.

He leaves the next day for a business trip to Panama. Years later she will tell me she always regretted not getting up and giving him a kiss.

A week later, Laura and Mom hang ornaments and tinsel on the Christmas tree standing in front of the big living room window looking out on Greenview Road. Light snow falls as they laugh and wonder what can be in the packages under the tree. A yellow VW Beetle turns the corner and drives past the house, slowing but not stopping. It's just like Dad's, only he's not due back from his trip until the next day.

I came home from college earlier in the day. I figure my dad comes home tomorrow and we'll go Christmas shopping the day after. Cutting it close, again. He has always been a last-minute Christmas shopper, and I follow in his footsteps. Our ritual goes like this: The day before Christmas he takes my brother and me to the Chicago Athletic Club for our workout and lunch, then ferries us to Marshall Fields an hour before the store closes so we can buy presents. I'm looking forward to our shopping expedition.

I think about last Christmas and the fun of the best family vacation we've ever had. We had gone to Panama, a place my dad was familiar with from his business trips. He had always loved the Latin culture, teaching himself Spanish and filling our house with the sounds of Latin music on the hi-fi. Case International de Panama S.A. was formed to do construction and foundation work in Central and South America, and my father was the logical choice to run it. When Vern Case retired in 1968, my dad and his good friend and partner, Mario Ospina, bought out his share. Mario ran the operations in Panama. That year he invited us to have Christmas dinner with him and his family at the luxurious Hotel El Panama. Nine of us sat at the circular dinner table, each with a personal waiter.

The next day, we all boarded the *Manana IV*, an exquisitely appointed sixty-foot boat my father and Mario frequently chartered to entertain clients. We headed south to some of the most renowned deep sea fishing waters in the world for six days.

It was early in the afternoon and the blistering sun hung above the sleek vessel. We were twenty miles off the coast of Colombia. "Do you see anything?" the dark man at the helm softly called in Spanish down to one of the crew.

"*Nada*," the man replied.

We'd been doing lazy circles in the Pacific for over seven hours. The glassy surface reflected a brilliant blue sky. Only one boat, a Colombian Navy patrol boat, had ventured remotely close to us, and that had been more than three hours ago. Mom lounged on a seat, smoking her ever-present unfiltered Chesterfields, her bright red lipstick staining the butt.

Laura leaned on the side of the boat, binoculars to her eyes, scanning the sea for any trace of fish. My dad napped on the rear deck. He had a *cerveza* in one hand and a high-tech Minolta camera in the other.

I hadn't seen him this relaxed for a long time. I knew that the business was having some trouble, but what I didn't know was that it was almost half a million dollars in debt and was being sued for $160 million for the faulty caissons that Case Foundation had installed for the 100-story John Hancock building in Chicago. No one could know that in 1970 Dad would take $20,000 out of their Panama account in order to invest in the corn and silver commodities markets, hoping to recoup enough to make the company solvent again. No one could know that the price of silver would drop so drastically that my father would lose $50,000 in a couple of days when the silver market collapsed. At that moment, all I knew was that we were having a perfect family vacation.

"Where are the fish?" I whispered to the young man standing vigilantly beside me. "Maybe they won't show."

My brother shrugged. Only God knew when or where the fish might appear.

Suddenly a sound like a combination of a finger snap and an ear-piercing "ping!" jerked us out of our lethargy. The line popped out of the clothespin holding it to the outrigger pole hanging off the starboard side.

The captain screamed, "Hook up!"

My dad bolted awake and lunged for the wickedly bending pole as line flew off the reel. He tossed his beer bottle over the side and shoved the brand new camera into the pocket of his shorts.

At least that's what he meant to do, but in the fog of excitement, before any of us could cry out, he had thrown his James Bond–class Minolta over the side and stuffed the half-full beer bottle, neck-first, in the pocket of his shorts. My brother and I erupted in laughter. Mom flicked the stub of her Chesterfield King into the ocean and pointed to the front of Dad's shorts, which were wet with beer. Of course, those damp drawers led to crude jokes and more laughter.

My father was, for him, in a rare state of indecision. Should he jump in the water and try to retrieve his camera? Or should he fight the fish? The fish was huge, the only one of any size to hit the bait all day. In those split seconds of hesitation he failed to set the hook and the monster—marlin or sailfish—spit it out. The line went limp.

"Goddamn it!" he shouted, throwing the pole to the deck. He pulled the empty beer bottle out of his pocket and hurled it as far as he could.

Maybe you knocked the fish out, Dad. The first words that came to mind died before they passed my lips. If I'd actually spoken them, he would no doubt have used me as bait.

The captain and crew guffawed along with the rest of us. My father relented, smiled, and reached into the ice chest. He handed cold beers to everyone except Laura, who was only twelve. As I swigged mine, I thought that in spite of losing a camera and a monster fish, this was still the best vacation we'd ever had.

It's eighty degrees when I leave L.A. to fly home that December day in 1970. When I land at O'Hare, the temperature is twenty-five. In spite of winter's chill, I go out that night with some friends and stay out late. I awake the next morning, December 22nd, and Laura is in bed with me, shivering and crying. My mother stands in the bedroom doorway, her face drained of all color, a stark contrast to her red-lacquered nails; a Chesterfield nestles between the first two fingers of her left hand. She chokes back tears.

"Your dad's dead. His secretary found him in his office this morning. They say he killed himself. The police are in the living room. Get dressed, please, and come talk to them with me."

Her one-suitcase lifeline has been rejected. The ropes tying us to the sturdy pier that was my father have been hacked away, setting us adrift in a sea of despair.

Vern Case and his son, Stan, fly in from California. Dad's oldest sister, Imogene, and her husband, Stu, come from Bakersfield to stay with us. Ironically, only five years earlier, my dad was the one who flew to California to comfort them when their twelve-year-old daughter, Jana, was killed in a horse jumping accident.

On Christmas Eve day, we sit in the front pew of the First Presbyterian Church. Rev. Tom Hinkin, a bear of a man, conducts the funeral. His red, bushy flattop seems to flame in the afternoon sunlight piercing the stained glass windows. There is no casket, no picture of my father. Only a handful of mourners have come to pay their respects. Suicide makes strangers of friends and neighbors. Later the place will be packed with joyful, hopeful families celebrating the birth of their savior, Jesus Christ. By then we will be long gone, the savior's name turned into a curse as we spiral farther into hell.

The family gathers at our house. No flowers perfume the room. No condolence cards lie on the coffee table. No one stops by with casseroles or salads or sympathy. My father's suicide is not fêted.

The men—I have been promoted to this tribe by default two days ago—huddle around the kitchen table, drinking scotch and smoking. We talk of Dad, telling funny stories instead of mourning. Stan tells how once he and his brother-in-law took a Case Foundation drilling rig from Chicago to someplace in Indiana to drill some test holes. The rig got stuck in the mud and it took them two days to get the thing out. I chime in with one about our fishing trip to Panama; howls of laughter erupt when I recount how my dad tossed his new camera overboard, thinking it was his empty beer bottle. The stories wind on and on.

Christmas Day dawns gray and cold, washed of all color. My brother, sister, Mom, and I sit in the living room. Slowly we open presents. Of course, I have nothing to give anyone—no last-minute shopping trip this year. Lackluster thank-you's and heavy hearts are all we can manage in the way of Christmas spirit.

When the presents have been opened and the gay wrappings tidied away, my mother hands me an envelope with my name on it. "This came in the mail yesterday."

It is a Case Foundation envelope, postmarked December 21 in Roselle, Illinois. I pull out the letter. Three hundred-dollar bills fall from the missive written in my father's hand. His customary steady cursive scrawls untidily across the paper. Two lines: *Casey—I sold some of your Hecla Mining shares. Please buy something for your mother and Laura.* These are my father's last words to us—to me. His suicide note. I throw it away.

When I'm alone, I write a note and enclose the money: *Mom, Merry*

Christmas. Please accept this from me and use it when you get to California to get something you really like. Think of it as a gift certificate. I love you very, very much. Casey.

In the week between Christmas and New Year's, Uncle Stan, my brother, and I drive to Wheaton to attend the coroner's inquest. In the Du Page County building, we're directed to a small, cramped, windowless room with auditorium-style seating, not unlike an operating theater in a medical school. We sit in padded seats, looking down upon a long gray metal table in the center of the gray-tiled floor below. Bare fluorescent lights hanging from the cheeseboard ceiling make the room seem even more depressing.

Three dark-suited men sit at the table. They pull name plates from their briefcases and place them on the table. Apparently this formality is supposed to convince us of their expertise. At a table set perpendicularly to the inquest committee's table sits Dr. Samuel K. Lewis, the coroner. The officials outnumber the family.

One of the committee members intones, "We are now ready to hear the matter of Grover Gauntt, Jr., deceased." He glances at us, acknowledging our presence. Then Dr. Lewis begins to speak. In cold, precise medical jargon he describes the facts and his findings. He holds up a plastic bag; the lights dull the finish of the snub-nosed .38 caliber handgun found next to "the subject's" body. Not my father. *The subject*. The gun had been purchased in a gun store in Chicago two days before Dad's body was discovered. He introduces a ballistics report that confirms that the bullet extracted from the deceased's skull was indeed fired from the gun in the bag and fingerprints on the gun match those of the subject.

I wonder if *the subject* returned from Panama early, or if he ever was in Panama. I will probably never know.

Numbness envelops me. It's the only way I can survive this grotesquery, the sterility of the proceedings. There is nothing of my father here, only gray men in a gray room in a gray day of death and loss.

Dr. Lewis stands and places a poster board on which a generic male head has been stenciled on an easel. Using a retractable pointer, he illustrates where the gun was pointed, the approximate distance of the barrel from the subject's temple when the gun was fired, and the circuitous path the bullet took inside the skull before lodging in the subject's brain.

No note was found at the scene.

I don't volunteer the fact that my dad mailed his last note to me, along with $300. It's none of their damned business.

He drones on, reading from the report filed by the Du Page County detective who had come to the house and interviewed my mother. Conclusion: The subject was having financial problems.

No one asks, "Why? What kind of man was he? Was he a good father?" No one says, "Boys, how are you coping with this tragedy?" There is not even a photo of *the subject*. No body, nothing. It's as if Grover Gauntt, Jr., never existed. And right about then, I wish he hadn't. Then I wouldn't be fighting to survive the devastation that his death has inflicted on me. I just want to get the fuck out of here.

The three suits unanimously accept the finding of "suicide by self-inflicted gunshot wound." Dr. Lewis is authorized to so certify on the death certificate. They stand, put their nameplates back into their briefcases, and leave. The whole proceeding has lasted seven minutes.

On December 29th, Dad's father, Bud, dies of a heart attack in El Paso, Texas. In a coma, he never learns that his son has predeceased him. They have been estranged for years. I wonder, had his health permitted, if he would have come to sit around our table and talk about his son. Probably not. His death is irrelevant to me, except as a passing coincidence. There is no ringing in of the new year, only trepidation of what lies ahead for each of us. Before I return to USC, I call Stan Lent, my fraternity brother who set up that first date with my first angel. He and Ron Guss are the only ones I tell of my father's suicide. Back at school, a few friends ask me about my Christmas vacation. I tell them my father died. If they are bold enough to ask how, I say, "Heart attack." Which is true. His heart did stop.

I fear that saying the word *suicide* will freak them out, that they won't understand it, which is complete bullshit. *I* don't understand it. *I'm* scared out of my mind. *I* have no fucking idea how I'm going to deal with it. So I lie. I lie about it for a long time. I'm good at that.

I cut all ties with my friends from childhood and high school. They are reminders of Itasca—of my father—and I want to erase that past. On the first anniversary of my father's suicide, Mom will say to us kids, "Well, we all know what today is, and we're not going to talk about it."

———

The end of the film flipped off the reel, flapping noiselessly as my tears flowed. I wasn't the only one weeping. In the forty years since my father's death, I had never seen my mother cry. Until now. What a revelation this night had been. I'd always had a nagging feeling that my mom was cold and aloof from her husband's death but had never had the guts to ask her. Now I realized how much she had reached out to him, trying to rally him as he sank deeper and deeper into despair.

She looked as if she couldn't believe that she'd finally let go of all the secrecy, the pain, that she'd held at bay with her "Let's get on with life" attitude.

At last the tears dwindled to a trickle. Hilary and Laura went into the kitchen to get dinner ready, and Mom and I were alone. I reached for her hand. "You have no idea how healing this is for me—for us—to talk like this, to hear and share these things."

She squeezed my hand. This lioness had spent the last forty years following her instincts and protecting her cubs.

I went on. "I'm so grateful to have you for my mother. You've never stopped showing me the way. I love you so much."

Then I told her about a dream I'd had a few nights earlier. "Dad and I were together somewhere. He looked good, fit, like he was in his forties. He complained of pain in his right shoulder. I put my hand in his armpit and pushed up. 'Is this where it hurts?'

"'Yeah, right there.'

"I told him it was probably his rotator cuff. Then I woke up."

She didn't say anything.

"The funny thing is that when I dreamed about Dad before Jimmy died, he was always silent, a background figure. We never touched, until in this dream I offered him free medical advice." A small smile showed that she appreciated my attempt to lighten the mood.

I went on to tell her about another dream a couple of months after Jimmy died, one in which my dad and I talked for the first time since Dad's death. That was a big goddamn deal! That seemed to be a turning point, and after that we talked whenever I dreamed about him, but we never touched. This dream deepened the cracks in the wall I had built around my emotions.

She smiled, as if she knew exactly what the dream meant.

Suddenly I thought I did, too. Matching her smile, I said, "I think he's around. He's driving by, and this time he's going to stop and pick you up. He's got a nice destination all picked out." My dad would have to cruise around the ether for four more months before my mom would be ready to climb into the passenger seat of their 1946 Ford Roadster, their honeymoon car with one suitcase in the trunk, and off they would go.

BROTHERS

I WAS BORN WITH boxing gloves, prepared for a fight with my brother, and if you asked Grover, or G.G. as we called him, he would have told you my mission in life was to torment him. We were a textbook case of sibling rivalry, two and a half years apart and extremely competitive. My brother was very neat and organized. I was not. He hated sharing his things, so I took to borrowing his clothes without asking, mainly because I liked his better. Of course, I never put them back exactly the way he liked, so we had plenty of fights over that, even though I told him he could borrow mine any time he wanted. I think the fact his little brother could fit into his things was an affront to his role as the dominant, older sibling. I was also a little better in school and sports (except wrestling, in which he excelled), and that irritated him.

He had another cross to bear, something I had nothing to do with. He was christened Grover Cleveland Gauntt III. Our dad was Junior, and his father was from an old Texas family that loved tradition. That's why my brother went by G.G. I mean, who wants to be named after a dead president?

My brother and I, however, shared one significant thing in common. We feared our father. I loved and respected my dad, but we were by no means buddies. There were two *modus operandi* in our house: Dad on the road and Dad at home. He travelled on business at least three days a week, and when Case opened its Panama office, he could be gone for a week or more at a time. When he was home, there was an edginess that filled the house. His rules were strict: dinner at the table, bring him up to speed on how we were doing in school, no television until homework was done, and hell to pay if my brother and I got into a fight or argument with one another, or the much greater offense of upsetting our sister, Laura, aka The Princess. My dad was quick with a hard slap on the ass, and occasionally took off his belt and used that. His stern look could make us quiver.

When G.G. was a sophomore in high school he made some remark about one of his female classmates who ratted her hair and wore heavy makeup. "She looks like a whore," he joked to his friends. That wisecrack made its way to her boyfriend, one of the "hard guys" who was older than us. He put the word out that he would track down my brother and beat the shit out of him.

Even though G.G. was afraid of Dad, he was more afraid of the threat, scared enough to tell our father about it.

Dad looked at him with cold blue eyes and said, "Don't worry about it. If he comes after you, I'll kill him. I've killed for less." That was the only thing he ever said that hinted at what two years in the South Pacific had done to him.

When our father was on the road, we had our dinner downstairs on TV trays and watched a show or two on television. Conversation was lighter. Sometimes we'd go to the Itasca Country Club for fish fry and hamburger nights. I used Dad's office to do my homework, played his stereo, and borrowed some of his clothes. G.G. and I shared the same small bedroom for many years until he finally moved down into the basement, which was divided into two parts. The improved part served as our family room, with a rug, a couch, chairs, a bar, and the television set. It also served as a poor excuse for a fallout shelter.

The fear of nuclear annihilation lurked all around us. In grade school we had nuclear attack drills at least twice a year, huddling under our desks as far away as we could get from the windows and putting our heads between our legs. A comedian would later add, "… and kiss our asses goodbye." This, of course, was utterly useless and absurd. We had watched, over and over, the film clips of atomic bomb tests on television and Super 8 movies in class: the fake towns in the desert, with mannequin moms working in the kitchen, mannequin kids playing in the yards, and mannequin dads watering the lawns or driving their Chevrolet convertibles with the tops down. The bomb, usually placed in a fake water tower in the center of town, would explode, instantly disintegrating everything within a five-mile radius. The resulting dust and vapor were sucked up into an enormous mushroom cloud rising into the thinnest layers of our atmosphere. Our puny Formica desks would be no match for that.

Almost every magazine and comic book in Mr. Lund's barber shop carried an advertisement for "How to build your own fallout shelter" or "Are you prepared in case of a nuclear attack?" In my opinion, our family was pathetically unprepared. My father was in the hole-digging business, for God's sake! We had a big backyard. How tough could it be for him to get some equipment and men over to the house, dig a hole, and construct a proper fallout shelter? We could easily get enough food and water to last the two weeks it would take for the radiation from the bombs to dissipate.

My dad pronounced a tiny five-by-seven storage room in our basement as "good enough" to keep us alive and not glowing in the dark. Oh, really? One problem surfaced right off the bat. It had a window. Even I knew that glass can't stop radiation. I politely suggested that we brick the window up, but my idea fell on deaf ears. One didn't press my father on matters involving war. My mother stocked this room with an inadequate amount of canned vegetables and fruits and tossed in a bottle of water. Those "provisions" wouldn't last two days.

Frustrated and angry, I made plans to speed over to the Lyons' place several doors down from us. When they built their new house in 1961 they installed a large fallout shelter. I'd beg to be let into their shelter, or break in if need be. But I knew there was no way I'd leave my folks. Instead, we'd cram in the closet and watch the radiation melt the window and seep into our soon-to-be grave. What was I worried about? We would only need provisions for a couple of minutes.

My mother finally stamped down upon my incessant protestations. "Look here!" she said. "If there's an attack, your father is going to be at work or off in Timbuktu or wherever, and you and your brother will be at school. So it's going to be me and your sister in this pathetic little room your father thinks is a fallout shelter. We're the ones who need to be worried, not you!"

Comforting to know I wasn't the only one freaked about it, and she was probably right. When the bombs did begin to fall, I'd be under my desk with all of my scared-shitless friends and teachers, our heads between our legs.

The Cuban Missile Crisis ramped up my fear. In October of 1962, we Americans were on tenterhooks for thirteen days, wondering whether Soviet missiles in Cuba, discovered and photographed by a U2 spy plane, would suddenly blast off and decimate the country.

President Kennedy ordered a naval blockade of the island to keep further Soviet military supplies from entering. He demanded that Soviet leader Nikita Khrushchev dismantle the missiles. In return, the United States would pledge not to invade Cuba.

The thought of being wiped out by either a direct hit or poisoned by radiation terrified me. I lay awake at night, wondering if I'd have time to run downstairs before the blast came, wondering how long we could live in the basement before we starved to death, wondering if our water would be contaminated and where we'd go to the bathroom.

The other part of the basement was unfinished, with concrete walls and floor. The washer, dryer, and Culligan water softener lived there, as did a huge oil-fired furnace and two large tanks of heating oil. This is where G.G. set up his own bedroom, away from me. I couldn't believe he did that. Not because I wanted him in my room, but because I was terrified of the furnace. I'd read about these kinds of furnaces blowing up. It didn't occur to me at the time that my bedroom was directly above the furnace, and when it blew it would be my ass hurled through the roof. I was just happy to have my own room.

G.G. was a late bloomer. He wrestled all four years in high school in the ninety-eight-pound weight class. During his senior year he starved himself and ran around in a rubber sweat suit on the day of the meet to lose an extra two or three pounds to make his weight class. From the backs of comic books, Charles Atlas had taught us to scorn ninety-eight-pound weaklings, but G.G. wasn't a weakling. He was a warrior and a very good wrestler.

He "taught" me to wrestle when he was a freshman, not because he wanted to teach his little brother something, but as punishment for my transgressions into his precious space. During one of our lessons, he locked his legs around me, essentially immobilizing me. He took off his shirt and tied my arms behind my back. I struggled and yelled as he tied me to a chair, but he ignored my pleas. "That'll teach you to mess with me," he snarled as he walked up the basement stairs and turned out the lights, leaving me captive in complete darkness next to the furnace. Two hours later, my mom came home and rescued me. I vowed that he would never imprison me again. I learned to wrestle in order to survive.

Years later, I realized that my brother, deep in his soul, has been a Zen Buddhist as long as I have known him, notwithstanding our childhood fights and our centuries-long heritage of Anglo-Saxon Protestant and Pagan upbringing that dates back to the highlands of Scotland and the lowlands of Lancaster, England. His roots go much farther back, deep roots he shared with Jimmy. My brother has dedicated the last forty years of his life to peace, healing, and helping mankind suffer less. I can admit—now—I didn't understand or respect his calling, his purpose, for a long time. I am happy and proud to say that today I do.

G.G. earned a business degree from USC and an MBA from the Wharton School of Business, and had his own real estate appraisal business for many years, but he found his passion and purpose in Zen Buddhism in the early 1970s. It led him to become a sensei, a master Zen teacher. He was given the name Genro, and "Grover" was retired. He has since been bestowed with the additional name, and honor, of Roshi. Genro and his Zen Peacemakers colleagues travel to places like Rwanda, Poland, Palestine, Congo, Serbia, and the Black Hills of South Dakota to help survivors heal from the genocides committed in those places and never forget that mankind has a sobering propensity to kill more of its own than any other species on the planet. Genro also leads several Street Retreats each year in major metropolises throughout the world where he takes small groups of suburbanites onto the streets, where they live as homeless people for several days. I refer to them as Hobo Holidays, to his chagrin.

It was on one of Genro's Bearing Witness Retreats where, unbeknownst to him, something took place that became the source of unspeakable rage and sorrow for me after Jimmy died. Jimmy spent his 2005–2006 senior year in London attending Queen Mary University to deepen his study of theatre and English literature. He travelled extensively throughout Great Britain and Europe at every possible opportunity. When Genro invited him to bear witness in Poland, Jimmy jumped at the chance. So in November, uncle and nephew found themselves inside Auschwitz-Birkenau, together with people of many faiths from all over the world. For a week, as he has done every year since 1996, Genro led the assemblage in meditations at the Nazi death camps where millions of European Jews were put to death during World War II.

One day Genro, Jimmy, and a hundred others sat in a circle in front of the Birkenau crematories. In spite of its horrific history, the area is surprisingly beautiful. Birches, maples, and sycamores surround the buildings, and the November chill had touched their leaves with a riot of golds, crimsons, and browns.

Genro needed to use the restroom, so he quietly left the circle to walk to the facilities a quarter of a mile away. When he came out, he noticed a huge tree in full color. The tree seemed to shimmer ethereally. As he stared at it, awed, suddenly—whoosh!—the tree lost all of its leaves, even though there was not even the slightest breeze. Every leaf had fallen at once in a shower of yellow.

He turned and saw Jimmy staring at the tree in amazement. Genro walked toward Jimmy.

"Thank you!" Jimmy said, his eyes wide and bright.

Genro shook his head. "Don't thank me. That was your work."

They walked back to the meditation circle in silence, both contemplating the strange things that seemed to happen whenever Jimmy was around.

Something else happened to Jimmy at that retreat. In their group was another James, a graduate student in philosophy at Oxford who had also trained as a shamanistic healer. There was a lot of walking involved in the trip and at one point Jimmy noticed pain in his abdomen. "Hold up, James. I've got a stitch in my side. Maybe I'm just tired and need to rest."

James looked at him intently. "It's not because of fatigue. You're carrying an entity, a spirit of someone who has passed. I can remove it for you when we get back to the hostel, if you like."

When they returned to the hostel where they were staying, they met in the autumn garden and James became more serious. "The spirit of your paternal grandfather is attached to you."

My father had died long before Jimmy was born and I rarely, if ever, spoke with Jimmy or Brittany about him. When Jimmy was ten, he found out more about his grandfather's death as we drove around with Genro and his two boys, who were visiting from Los Angeles. Inexplicably, Genro's seven-year-old blurted out, "Grandpa Grover shot himself!" Jimmy gave me a stunned, questioning look. I was livid. I didn't want Jimmy to know that, at least not until he was older. I didn't want him to carry that image around in his head. I also deeply regretted not being the one to tell him.

Jimmy told Shaman James how his grandfather died and instructed him to go ahead with the detachment.

James held a crystal. He blew to the east, south, west, and north and called on the spirit of an eagle. In five minutes, the ceremony was over. The pain did not go away, but Jimmy, not wanting to hurt his friend's feelings, said, "Thanks. I notice a remarkable difference."

Jimmy returned to London and fell in love with Sara, another USC student studying abroad. At the end of the term, Sara left for Chile to continue her studies in Santiago, and Jimmy chased after her. Two months later he was back in Solana Beach with a broken heart. While he was home he confided in Brittany about the shaman and the detachment ceremony. At some point I heard about it and tried to bring up the topic with Jimmy, but he was uncharacteristically reticent. "It's nothing. I don't want to talk about it." He made no mention of my dad being attached to him, and I gave it no more thought.

Before he moved back up to Los Angeles to pursue his writing career, he spent a lot of time in the finished attic of our house where he liked to write when he was home. Boxes of family scrapbooks and photographs filled much of the space. Jimmy found and read several letters my father had written to his sweetheart Barbara and his parents during the war. Pictures of Jimmy's grandfather as a boy, a soldier, a young father, and a middle-aged man, it all fascinated him. Strange emotions came over him. He felt a need to be more available to his grandmother Barbara and reach out to her, which he did. He told Brittany all this but made her promise not to tell me, saying, "It will freak Dad out."

Three months after Jimmy was killed, Brittany came over for dinner. "You know Jimmy met that shaman in Poland," she said. "Did he ever tell you about the spirit that was attached to him?"

"I remember Jimmy shutting down when I tried to bring it up. He later sent me an e-mail apology and made the thing with the spirit and the shaman out as no big deal."

Brittany went on. "Well, the shaman told him that your dad's spirit had attached itself to Jimmy and he did a ceremony that was supposed to remove it. Jimmy said it didn't work." Brittany didn't recall if James or Jimmy thought the attachment was a good or bad thing. "Jimmy told me that before and after the Poland trip he felt a peculiar connection with your dad. Jimmy was aware of something around him, and he was compelled to learn more. Jimmy was obsessed with finding out everything he could about your father."

This scared the hell out of me! The idea of this dark, silent, depressed man who blew his brains out sitting on my son's shoulder and somehow advising him sent all that old dread, fear, and anger roaring back into my brittle psyche.

After Brittany left, Hilary and I talked some more about Jimmy's "possession." I don't remember much about that conversation, but later she would say, "I hadn't seen you that angry in ages. Do you remember what you said?"

I shook my head. I had blocked the words out as I wandered into a dark place I had never wanted to go back into.

"You said, 'What the hell is my dad doing hanging around Jimmy? If he had something to do with Jimmy's death, I don't think I can live with that.'"

I took her in my arms, tears filling my eyes. Her warmth and love encircled me, letting me know that all would come right—maybe someday.

I began to see a psychologist six weeks after Jimmy's death. I knew deep in my core I needed help to absorb his loss as well as to finally confront my father's suicide. My work with Dr. Frank Altobello—Dr. A as he likes to be called—has been enormously helpful to me. The Tuesday following our conversation with Brittany, Dr. A and I talked about Jimmy's experience in Poland and my grave concerns regarding the spirit attachment.

"Why don't you ask Genro if he knows where Shaman James is?" he suggested. "Talk to him and get his side of the story. There's a powerful connection among your father, Jimmy, and you. We need to see where this is going."

On Wednesday, I called my brother in New York and explained my quest to track down this Shaman James.

"I'll see if I can find his contact information, but without his last name, it might be tough to do," Genro promised. "I'll let you know what I find out."

"Did you have any idea this stuff with Dad's spirit was going on?" I asked.

"No. Jimmy never spoke of this shaman or told me what had occurred between them."

"If Dad had anything to do with Jimmy's death—"

Genro interrupted me. "Casey, this possession would have only been a good thing. Dad would only be around Jimmy to protect and look after him."

I wasn't convinced. If hanging around in Jimmy was such a good thing, then why would James have offered to detach the spirit? Confusion engulfed me as I sank deeper into despair.

Genro left again for Poland on October 30, 2008, to lead the next Bearing Witness Retreat. On Saturday, November 1, he sent me this e-mail.

"I found him. He's James Powell. Good luck. Hope your Halloween was great. All love, Grover." He included James's e-mail address.

Laura called me from her home in Switzerland the next morning. During our conversation I mentioned to her that I'd been listening a lot to James Taylor's rendition of "River," a Joni Mitchell song. "Every time I hear it, it makes me cry, particularly when he sings, "I made my baby cry, I made my baby say goodbye. Oh, I wish I had a river, I could skate away on." Tears filled my eyes. "God, Laura, I couldn't protect Jimmy. I couldn't protect my baby!"

She sent me an e-mail later that same day. "Oh my goodness, I haven't cried so hard since I don't know when as I was listening to 'River'… I get it, I really do… but there aren't any frozen rivers in San Diego and you can't just skate away. You stay there and take care of Hilary and Brittany. They need you more than ever and more than you know. But I understand. All my love."

My sister's antennae were up, not uncommon among survivors of suicide. I wasn't contemplating taking my life—that option wasn't on the table. My father had already used that way out, and the last thing I was going to do was put my family through more hell than we were already living. But I was mighty low. I'd hit bottom in my shaft of desolation.

And that is when my portal opened.

THE LETTER

There are more things in heaven and earth, Horatio, than are dreamt of in your philosophy.

Hamlet, Act 1, Scene 5

SAT IN MY law office the morning after the call with my sister. I was functioning, but just barely. I was finally able to put in a full day at my law practice, an improvement from the four-hour mornings that were all I could handle in the several weeks after Jimmy died. My partners at the Allen Matkins firm were wonderful. They swooped in immediately and picked up the load I could not carry.

A knock on the door roused me. Shelley Malone, my assistant, entered as if she were walking on eggshells. She said, "An Emily Sue Buckberry called. Said she knew you many years ago in Coalwood, West Virginia. She has something you left behind and thought you might want it. Here's her cell number." She put the pink message slip on my desk and left.

I stared at the phone message. Who was this woman and why was she contacting me after all these years? What could she possibly have that I would want now? I remembered Coalwood very well, but the Buckberry name meant nothing to me. I tried to busy myself with other things, but after considering the message for an hour, still hesitant about the wisdom of contacting a stranger, I dialed her cell phone.

"Emily Buckberry," a staticky, cheerful voice said.

"Uh, this is Casey Gauntt. You left a message for me?"

"Hey, Casey! I'll be damned. You probably don't remember me, but my mom and I lived on the third floor of the Clubhouse the summer you worked in Coalwood."

She was right. I didn't remember her. Coalwood had been forty years ago.

She must have sensed my confusion, because she said, "You used to play your guitar on the porch and sing. Sometimes we'd all sing along."

A vague image of long brown hair, glasses, and a smile hovered in my mind. "I remember," I fibbed.

"I told your assistant that you'd left something behind in Coalwood. As handsome as you are, she probably thinks it was a baby."

We both laughed.

She went on. "When you left Coalwood, I was bummed that I didn't get to say goodbye. I went past your room and saw a letter and an empty Case Foundation Company envelope addressed to you lying next to a wastebasket outside your room. I picked them up and scanned the first couple of paragraphs. It was a letter to you from your father. The envelope was marked Personal. Your father had written about problems Case was having on its shaft job for the Olga Mining Company, and I was afraid that—Coalwood being a company-owned town and all—if that letter got around town, there'd be big problems. I thought, *Casey should have ripped this up or something. Did he really mean to throw it away?*"

I didn't remember ever getting a letter like that from my father. He didn't write letters to me.

She went on. "So I kept it, intending to send it on to you. But I got sidetracked with graduate school and life in general. The other day, I was going through some boxes and found the letter. I Googled you, called your San Diego office, and here we are."

She chattered on. "So, Casey, are you married?"

"Yes," I grunted, dreading the next, inevitable question.

"Any kids?"

I choked back tears as I recounted Jimmy's senseless death three months earlier. I'm sure she spoke words of condolence, but I barely heard them.

Her voice was somber, all her cheerfulness sucked away, as she said, "I'd like to send this letter to you, if you want it. What's your address?"

Did I want it? Emily hadn't asked me anything about my father. This woman had opened a door—did I want to walk in? I wasn't afraid—three months earlier I'd already experienced the worst thing that can happen—but my dad had caused me and my family so much pain. Emily did say the letter was beautiful.... "Sure." I gave her my home address and we ended the call.

Gradually an overwhelming sense that something very strange and powerful was afoot came over me. The air around me filled with electricity and the hairs on the back of my neck stood straight up as goose bumps covered my body. Something was happening. I cried hard for several minutes. I'd never before experienced anything like what was now coursing through my body. I didn't tell Emily I'd been thinking a lot about my father the last few weeks and how he had come into Jimmy's life. Something was happening and it had begun during the summer of 1968.

Jimmy and Casey Gauntt, Continental Divide, Colorado 1992

Coalwood, West Virginia 1968, L to R front row: Charles "Tafon" Hylton, Herbert "Hub" Alger, Casey "Long Ass" Gauntt, and Gene "Ringo" Kirk ; L to R back row: Zachary "Squirrel" Fleming, James "Muss" Alger, Marty Valeri, and Pete Burnett

Franz Joseph Glacier, South Island, New Zealand 2005, Casey, Brittany, Hilary, and Jimmy

Four Generations 2010, Casey, Brittany Kirby, Wyatt Kirby, and Barbara Gauntt

Grover (aka Roshi, Genro, and G.G.) and Casey 2012

Honolulu 1967   Grover, Mom, Casey, Laura, and Dad

Casey and My First Angel, Hilary 1972

Jimmy and Hilary Zion National Park, May 2008

Hilary and Casey Christmas 1992

Rod Knutson's Gauntt-Kirby family portrait (2006) as it normally appears

The same painting with Jimmy all lit up on the night of "The Jimmy" scholarship awards at Torrey Pines High School, June 2013. Casey is seated with a book and Hilary is standing in the doorway

Jimmy and brother-in-law Ryan Kirby, Kulik River, Alaska 2006

Jimmy, The Ghost Writer with Princess 2007

Jimmy & Laura (Laura is Jimmy's Aunt - Casey's Sister)

Jimmy and Laura Gauntt Butie, Harrod's London 2006

Hunter and Wyatt Kirby on Jimmy's Bench, San Elijo Lagoon, Solana Beach
August 9, 2015

Dad, Mom, and best man Jack Fredericks, Wedding Day, March 6, 1946
Los Angeles

Anthony "Tony" Ortega and Jimmy 2002

Laura, Casey, and Dad, Panama 1969

Steve Date getting ready to film Casey tell his story of The Letter, Coalwood, WV,
October 2009

Jimmy and Henri, 2001 Torrey Pines High School

Emily Sue Buckberry and Casey, The Clubhouse, Coalwood, WV 2009

Casey "Pa" and Hunter Kirby unveiling the tattoo August 9, 2013

Jimmy at the finish of the 2007 Los Angeles Marathon

Brittany and Jimmy August 18, 2007

"Hey Britt, you're pregnant! And it's a boy!"

COALWOOD

O N JUNE 9, 1968, my flight landed in Charleston, West Virginia. As I pulled my suitcase from the baggage carousel, a young man with black hair and a swarthy complexion strode up. He wore tan pants and a long-sleeved shirt. A flat-billed railroad engineer's cap perched on the back of his head. "Hi. I'm Tim Bowman, but everybody calls me Mex," he said, sticking out his hand.

I shook it. "I'm Casey."

"Figured so," Tim said. "Boss's kid, right?"

I nodded, wondering if that fact would be held against me. Tim didn't seem to care one way or another. "Come on. It's a long drive to Coalwood," he said, leading the way to a beige pickup with the Case Foundation Company logo emblazoned on the driver's door.

On the two-hour drive, I learned that Tim had been born and raised in Coalwood, the middle child in a family of three boys and three girls. He was my age, eighteen, and had just graduated from Big Creek High School in War, a couple of towns over the mountain.

Tim drove casually, one hand on the wheel, his left elbow crooked over the open window. I was transfixed by his Southern drawl as he laughed and joked and asked me questions about living in the big city. He reminded me of a younger Sheriff Andy Taylor from *The Andy Griffith Show*, which I had watched religiously since it first appeared on television in 1960. We swapped stories as we cruised along. By the time we arrived in Coalwood, we were friends.

Coalwood, in the southwest corner of West Virginia near the Kentucky border, became famous in 1998 for being the home of Homer Hickam, Jr., known as Sonny to his friends, whose fledgling experiments with rocketry in the late 1950s led him to later write a book about the town and his and his friends' experiences. *Rocket Boys* was a huge best seller and later was made into the movie *October Sky,* which starred Jake Gyllenhall as Sonny and Chris Cooper as his father. Mr. Hickam, Sr., was the superintendent of the Olga Mining Company coal mines buried deep below the town.

During our call Emily Buckberry asked me if I'd seen *October Sky.* Hilary and Jimmy had gone to see the film soon after its release. When I got home she said, "We just saw a movie that I think takes place in that town you worked in the summer after high school." The next day I went to see the movie and bought the book. I was shocked that a movie had been made about such a small, tucked away-from-everything town. Emily also told me she and Sonny grew up together and were close friends, and that she was hired to work on the film as a dialogue consultant. "The director, Joe Johnston, didn't want the actors to sound like they were from the film *Deliverance,*" she explained.

As he made clear in *Rocket Boys,* Sonny had a less-than-warm relationship with his father, a no-nonsense mine boss who believed in hard work, company loyalty, and sticking with what you knew. So familiar with the depths of the earth, he couldn't understand why his son would want to waste time on things that went up into the sky. Even Sonny's numerous awards from science fairs didn't faze him. However, when the boys brought home a gold medal from the national science fair, Homer Sr. came down to the slag heap to see what they were up to.

Mr. Hickam had black lung disease, a consequence of his many years of exposure to coal dust. As Sonny and his pals prepared to launch their latest creation, Sonny turned to his dad and said, "You launch it."

Mr. Hickam put his thumb on the toggle and pushed. Flames shot from the rocket and it rose majestically. Mr. Hickam got so excited that he lost his breath. Sonny put his arm around him to hold him up. It was the first close moment ever for Sonny and his father.

Later Sonny would say, "So in a lot of ways—actually in all the ways— I wrote that book for that final scene: to write about the moment that I had with my father growing up. I never had a moment like that before, and never had a moment after, but for that moment my father and I connected and, ultimately, that's what *Rocket Boys* is about."

It wasn't until ten years after reading Sonny's book that I discovered Coalwood was the crucible for my moment with my father and my return to the light; ironic, since I spent most of that summer in a hole hundreds of feet below ground.

Between my senior year of high school and my freshman year at the University of Southern California I worked for Case Foundation on a job in Coalwood. Case had been hired by the Olga Mining Company to install a two thousand-foot ventilation shaft for a new section of its coal mines. This was a very odd job for Case to take on. Its specialty was constructing deep foundations for skyscrapers such as the two-hundred-foot deep caissons sunk in 1966 for the one hundred-story John Hancock Building in Chicago known as "Big John."

I had begun working for Case the summer after sixth grade. My brother and I painted the seven-foot fence that encircled the ten-acre headquarters property in the Chicago suburb of Keeneyville, laboring for six or seven hours a day for fifty cents an hour, a lavish sum in 1962. Not yet men of height, we erected a scaffold so our brushes could reach to the top of the fence.

One morning I was sitting on the scaffold, painting a section of the fence near the office building, when my mother's father came out of the building, dressed, as usual, to the nines in his hand-tailored three-piece dark gray suit and black wingtips with metal studs in the heels. His heels chirped on the concrete as he marched across the parking lot, his face stone serious. He didn't bother with a greeting. "Casey, don't ever let me catch you sitting down again while you're working. It makes you look lazy. If you need to, get down on one knee, but never on both knees. If you're too tired to work, go home." He turned on his heel and marched back into his office.

The following summers I worked at many different jobs—carpenter, welder, lathe operator, laborer—but always during slow times, keeping in mind my grandfather's admonishment, I picked up a broom and swept the shop floor, put tools away, or cleaned parts without being asked. I learned at a very young age how to work hard and do a good job. I never allowed anyone to think I didn't pull my weight, even if I shared the owner's blood.

Tim helped me get settled in the Clubhouse, a splendid three-story boarding house and hotel built in the early 1900s. Enormous white pillars framed the porch and entrance. Junior Chapin and his wife, Carol, ran the place, both employed by Olga. As I followed Mrs. Chapin to my room on the second floor, she chattered away like we were old friends. "We live here in the hotel, you know. We have two teenage daughters, Kim and Theresa. You'll get to know them real quick. I make breakfast every morning, and I'll make sure you have a good lunch to take with you. Dinner is at five-thirty sharp."

As I unpacked, I wondered what it would be like living in a company town where every house, every business, every person was owned or employed by the mine. It wouldn't take long to find out.

The jobsite was a few miles outside of town on the side of a hill above Mudhole Holler. The day shift crew met at the Clubhouse around seven-thirty, and we drove up to the job in the company's four-wheel drive Jeeps. It was a "two-smoke ride." I usually bummed unfiltered Camels from one of the crew members everyone called The Greek.

I considered myself reasonably fit, but my first shift in the shaft made me realize that a passion for golf and gymnastics couldn't prepare me—or anyone—for the rigors of underground mining. I got kitted out in my yellow, waterproof suspendered pants and coat, strapped the battery pack for my miner's lamp to my waist, settled the wide-brimmed metal hard hat on my head, and stepped into the skip, a metal can a few feet square that acted as a crude elevator to drop us down to the bottom of the shaft. The sides came barely above our waists. Tafon, Hub, and Rat, all Coalwood boys, rode down with me.

"Keep all the body parts you wanna keep inside this here skip," Rat informed me, "or whatever hangs out will come back a bloody stump."

Fear rose in me as the skip began to drop. I pressed my arms close to my sides. This mine would not claim any of my body parts if I could help it. The skip picked up speed, plunging four hundred feet to the bottom of the shaft, where I'd spend the next eight hours. The jagged rock walls blurred as we plummeted past.

The skip slowed and stopped. I hitched up my britches and stepped out into darkness pierced only by the headlamps we wore. My first day of work had begun.

I was handed a pneumatic drill—a jackhammer. My job was to drill holes into solid rock to accommodate the sticks of dynamite that would shatter rock and deepen the shaft. The jackhammer was about two feet in length and weighed sixty pounds. Tafon Hylton, the foreman, showed me how to clip a five-foot drill bit into the business end.

"Hold it as far above your head as you can, and keep it tight to the rock," he instructed. Fortunately, I had grown quite a bit the past couple of years and was about six foot two and a whopping one hundred fifty pounds. I set the bit against the rock and pressed the trigger.

Oh, shit! It felt like my teeth were going to shake out of my gums. The noise was ferocious. As I drilled my way down into the two-inch diameter hole, the work got a little easier and I learned some tricks of the trade, thanks to Rat Kirk, the only guy on the crew skinnier than me, with an Adam's apple big enough to rival Johnny Appleseed's. Once I got the drill handles down to chest level, I'd throw one of my legs over the drill to add more weight to force it down. When it worked its way a little lower, I sat on it.

More than once the drill bit would suddenly bind up in the hole and I'd get bucked off the drill like a cowboy tossed from a bull's back, slamming into the wall and getting pretty banged up. The other miners guffawed, thinking that was about the funniest thing they'd ever seen. I'd struggle to my feet, shrug, and do it all over again.

Drilling through solid rock, even with water-cooled drills, created a blinding swirl of dust. The solution? Red Man chewing tobacco. I'd put a big chaw of that in my jaw and as I breathed in through my mouth, the slug of wet tobacco acted like a filter and trapped some of the dust—at least in theory. Of course, it never dawned on me that I was swallowing the dust, along with the nicotine, which made me feel like I could work forever and never get tired.

My mom would have been horrified at such a dirty habit. I could almost hear her: "If everybody jumped off a cliff, would you jump, too?" Well, I felt like I was figuratively jumping off a cliff when I climbed into the skip, and if I was old enough to do a man's work, I was old enough to pick up a man's habits.

The noise pounded us from all sides, deafening, suffocating, exploding, and crashing off the solid granite walls of the fourteen-foot-wide shaft. Compressors pumped air to four drills, creating a cacophony as we miners punched sixty firing holes in the rock floor. I would soon learn that the noise never stopped. Never.

Eight weary hours later, ears ringing from the constant hammering of the drills, bodies drenched in sweat, we packed ourselves like sardines inside the skip and began the slow, cautious ascent from this hell-pit. Water seeped constantly from the walls of the shaft above us, pouring off the brims of our metal helmets and running inside the collars of our heavy jackets. Even our waterproof coats couldn't keep us dry. The seeping water added to my misery.

After we passed through a maze of cables, hoses, and steel supporting the jaws of a gigantic metallic shovel, the skip surged upward, cementing our boots to the floor. The noise dissipated as we rocketed toward a dime-sized circle of bluish-gray light, the doorway out of hell. Large droplets of water smashed into my face, turning into rivulets that carved tracks through the rock dust caked on my forehead and smooth adolescent cheeks. I wiped the muck from my eyes as turquoise light surrounded us, dancing upon the cavern walls retreating beneath.

I looked down through the receding murk. Through the damp, dust-filled air, tiny pinpricks of yellow light, the rapidly vanishing headlamps of the second shift heading into the hole we'd just left, winked up at me, like lightning bugs that filled the muggy summer nights in suburban Chicago with magic. I was a long way from Chicago. I wanted to scream, "How the hell did I end up here?" The noise was so damned loud, I could have shouted at the top of my lungs and the three local men crammed in the bucket with me wouldn't have heard a thing.

The biggest deterrent, though, was that over the years, I had learned not to show fear—or any other honest emotion. Emotion was something my father and grandfather seldom expressed, and they seemed to hold those who did in low esteem.

Looking up, I shielded my eyes from the blinding light that gradually softened to pale blue as we hurtled toward the surface. The skip slowed. The metal grate that covered the mouth of the shaft to keep unwary pedestrians from a long, long fall rolled back. The grizzled guardian, his long, dirty hair dangling around his face, permitted us to pass through, greeting us with a wide grin. His few remaining teeth were stained by years of tobacco and neglect, each gap in his gums a story. Our Top Man, as he was called, had recently been released from prison, having served ten years for second-degree murder. "Only one they ever done got me on," he beamed.

Tafon, Hub, Rat, and I hopped out into the relative quiet of the surface, and the grate rolled back into place. I took off my hard hat and knew that if I looked in a mirror, my forehead would stand out whitely, a stark contrast to the rest of my face, which was covered in grit and sweat. I switched off my headlamp and unbuckled the battery pack. I couldn't wait to shed the waterproof gear and feel the breeze on my skin.

Five days earlier I had celebrated my graduation from Lake Park High School in suburban Chicago. Now I asked myself what the fuck I was doing in Coalwood, West Virginia, working with a bunch of miners. I wondered if I would ever become one of them. But at least I had survived the first day.

One evening after dinner, when I'd been in Coalwood less than a week, I was sitting on the wide porch of the Clubhouse with some of the boys, occasionally shouting something at another bunch sitting on the steps of the Big Store across the road. The setting sun touched the tops of the deep green, almost blue, Appalachia hills that protected this tiny coal town, sending a warm golden light over the land. It made me feel that anything was possible, including surviving the Case Foundation shaft project.

I looked up to see Tim Bowman sauntering down the road. "Hey, buddy," he called, "take a walk with me. I want you to meet my folks."

I hopped off the porch and Tim and I strolled down the middle of Main Street. The night shift workers had gone down in the mines a couple of hours earlier. Those lucky enough to be topside to enjoy the balmy summer evening sat with their feet up on porch rails, tossing out friendly greetings.

As we passed the turnoff to Snakeroot Hollow, Tim said, "That's where the colored live."

I was surprised by his casual reference to segregation. I didn't consider myself prejudiced, but to be honest, the only Negroes, as African Americans were called at the time, I'd actually known while growing up were Carrie Fowler, who cleaned our house, and Russell Allen, my grandfather's and father's chauffeur.

Though the rest of the country was being torn apart by race riots in the aftermath of the assassination of Dr. Martin Luther King, Jr., Coalwood seemed oblivious to outside struggles. For a moment I wondered if the blacks had been required to keep to themselves or if they preferred to gather together. Then I reminded myself that Coalwood was part of the South, and that it wasn't my place to judge how folks here lived.

A hundred yards later Tim and I came to Mudhole Branch Road, which forked off to the right, leading to the shaft job. We took the left fork up Frog Level Row, a string of fifty cookie-cutter, single-story wood-framed houses on lots the size of postage stamps. Originally, they had been painted white, but in the dusk they hunkered like gray ghosts, their clapboards having surrendered long ago to the coal dust, which hunted down every exposed surface. Like most of the other houses in town, these were owned by the Olga Mining Company and rented out to the miners.

A tiny stream flowed through the hollow. "Looks harmless now," Tim said, "but after a gully washer, that crick can rise up ten feet or more. That's how come some of the houses are up on stilts." He turned toward a small two-story house. "Home, sweet home," he said.

Tim held the weathered screen door open for me as we entered the family room. The remnant odors of dinner, something fried, hung close to the low ceiling, mingling with the dense cloud of cigarette smoke. The only light in the tiny room came from the nineteen-inch black-and-white television that sat in one corner. A hand rose above the back of a large recliner that dominated the room. The red tip of a Camel glowed between the stubs of two fingers.

"Dad, I want you to meet somebody," Tim said.

His words were answered by a wet, raspy hack erupting from the bowels of the chair. Tired springs creaked from the upheaval as Tim and I sidestepped around the recliner into the room. I repressed the urge to stare as I looked at a gray skeleton that seemed to be struggling to escape the overstuffed cushions of the faux leather La-Z-Boy. Black pools had replaced Mr. Bowman's eyes. The taut skin where his cheeks had once been sucked against his back molars, outlining them as if the flesh had been pasted over the teeth.

"Pleased to meet you," he whispered, extending a skeletal hand.

I took his right hand in mine, wary that even my light touch might break the fragile bones. He struggled out of the chair. I was aghast. There couldn't have been ninety pounds of flesh on his six-foot frame. Once-blue denim shirt and trousers, now faded to white from thousands of washings, hung on him like old clothes fluttering around an autumn scarecrow. He was fifty-three, going on seventy-nine.

Later Tim would tell me that his father, like so many other men, had been forced to retire from mining when he contracted black lung disease from breathing the dust in the years before respirators became mandatory. He received a disability stipend of just over a hundred dollars a month.

Everyone in town knew that my grandfather and father ran Case Foundation, and I was a little surprised when things went fairly smoothly with the other members of the crew. I suppose working all those previous summers for Case in Illinois had prepared me better than I imagined to work with hard men who didn't have time to babysit a kid with the silver spoon sticking out of his mouth. I had worked a lot around guys older than me who came from widely diverse backgrounds. By the time I was twelve, I had learned to swear with the best (or worst) of them and how to fit in.

They didn't let me off scot-free, though. One day I was topside. "Hey, Casey! Move that Jeep!" someone shouted, pointing to one of our transport vehicles.

"Right away!" I yelled back. I jumped in the Jeep and fired it up. Suddenly I heard this loud tttkkkktttktkkktkk behind me. I looked over my shoulder. An enormous eastern diamondback rattlesnake was coiled on the seat, its spade-shaped head weaving back and forth.

I flew out of the Jeep and dove to the ground. When I dared to look up, I saw the entire crew laughing their asses off, falling down and rolling around holding their sides. Sheepishly, I got to my feet, dusted myself off, and went back to what I had been doing before I fell for their prank.

Another time I was asked to move a tractor. I climbed up into the driver's seat, turned the key, and pressed the starter, but nothing happened. I got out and lifted the seat to check the battery. Sitting on one of leads to the battery was a blasting cap used to ignite the dynamite we stuffed into the holes drilled at the bottom of the shaft. If the engine had fired, it could have blown my ass off—literally. This time there was no one around watching.

Had they indeed been just practical jokes? Little tests to see how I'd take it and find out what I'd do? Thinking back, I realize if I had ever tried to pull any sort of rank with these guys, they could have easily arranged "accidents" and they wouldn't have thought twice about it.

Later that summer Tim confided in me. "Those first few weeks you were here? Somebody—I'm not sure who, and I don't know if they worked for Case or Olga—sneaked into your room and went through your stuff all the time."

"Why the hell would somebody do that?" I answered, outraged at this violation of my privacy.

Tim shrugged. "Just checkin' you out, I guess, tryin' to figure out what you're doin' in Coalwood."

"Like I'm some kind of spy?"

Tim shrugged again. He had no answers. Neither did I.

That summer, I worked hard and I played hard. Shortly after I arrived, Tim invited me to join the Coalwood softball team. I was pretty proud to put on the uniform that had "Case Foundation" written across the shirt. "But I'm not askin' you because you're the boss's kid. And nobody from Case told me we had to invite you to join. We did it just because you fit in," Tim said.

I felt that way, too. Most people there had accepted me easily, and they were the friendliest, most open, fun people I'd ever been around.

Three-two beer was legal for those of us eighteen and older, and we drank a lot of it. On nights we weren't running bases and hoping for home runs, we'd drive over to Welch and shoot rats at the dump. Rats are like moths, drawn to light. We'd pull the car to the edge of the dump, switch on the headlights, and climb on the hood. Hundreds of rats charged toward the car as we blasted away with our .22 caliber rifles. That's what I call fun.

My dad came to visit me late that summer. We had dinner and he spent the night in the Clubhouse. The next day he joined me at the jobsite, an alien draped in his dark blue suit. The crew snapped to, almost saluting when he showed up. My father naturally commanded that level of respect from tough men. He paid little attention to me. Inside I was beaming.

As he got ready to leave for Chicago, he took me aside. "Casey, before you get home, do me a favor. Get a haircut and don't chew tobacco in front of your mother."

As August wound down toward September, I felt sad that my time here was ending. Coalwood and the shaft job had been real learning experiences, at least a couple of doctorates' worth. It was transforming—I arrived as a boy and left as a man. I would miss Tim and all my new friends. I would miss the town and its friendly people. Yet a new adventure loomed: college at USC and a new life in Los Angeles. On August twenty-fourth, as I boarded the plane that would take me home, I never imagined that I'd have anything more to do with Coalwood or anyone who lived there.

INTO THE LIGHT

O N THE SATURDAY after Emily Buckberry's call, Hilary and I went with Brittany, Ryan, and my mother to Del Mar Beach. The Santa Ana winds had blown in a perfect day: cloudless sky, a sea the color of sapphires, and temperatures in the high seventies. Britt and I paddled out past the breakers on boogie boards. I had a plastic zipper-lock bag with some of Jimmy's ashes in it tucked into my trunks. As we sat upright on our boards and rode the rolling swells, I tipped the ashes into the ocean he loved so much, watching as they formed a gray cloud that spread beneath our feet. Several yards away a mother seal lay on her back, cradling her baby on her stomach. Scores of pelicans and seagulls dive-bombed a school of bait fish. Surfers rode the clean swells that rose into breaking waves. Even with the remnants of death spreading around us, life seemed to be reminding us that there is never truly an end to it.

Around three, Mom was ready to go home. "I'll run her home," I told Hilary. "Then I'll be back. Anything you want?"

Sadness haunted her eyes as she replied, "We're fine. See you after a bit."

I dropped Mom off and decided to swing by our house and check the mail. Inside the box was a priority mail package from Emily. I took it inside and tossed it on the counter. I hesitated to open it, to see my father's handwriting once again. There it lay while I fiddled around for a bit in the kitchen. At last I tore the strip off the package and pulled out the Case Foundation Company envelope postmarked June 19, 1968. The envelope itself was as pristine as the day it had been sealed. I knew right then I had never received it because my habit was to open every letter by tearing off one end. The flap on this one had been opened carefully. Who had intercepted it, read it, and tossed it next to the wastebasket outside my room after I'd left? Would I ever find out? Did it really matter?

Emily had attached a note. "Here are some words from your dad that might help sustain you as a bereaved father. It surely can't do anything but comfort you to be reminded of how much you were loved as a son."

I drew out the letter. My father's neat handwriting spread across both sides of the page.

Grover C. Gauntt, Jr.

June 19, 1968

Dear Casey,

Well, we miss you already. I borrowed your clubs and met Buz Paschen at Bob O' Link yesterday. It rained all day and we didn't play. GG was in your room this AM looking for a black shoelace; fortunately, I had a spare. Joey, Carter and Dave were over last nite to get your amplifier, or return it, I don't know which; again the matter revolved around the rain.

I hope you find your work interesting and contribute to the project. We have lost a lot of time on the job due to many factors. Leadership has been one of the big factors. We have a good contract, but it does not cover stupidity. The three explosions we have had on the job nicked into our hopeful profit and caused us serious delays in production. The schedule precipitated management of Olga Coal Co. to pressure us. They had some good arguments and analyzed our problem accurately a long time ago. I sent down what I hope is a reformed Jim Walton and he has been effective. I thought it well you go to Coalwood—you might learn from a bad situation. Your leadership qualities might be contagious. Don't ever throw in the towel—make the most of a bad situation. Don't join them—beat them.

I don't consider myself as successful; therefore, I'm not going to preach to you. I have knocked around a lot on some tough construction problems and have a lot of experience, some good, some bad. Others have to judge me. I really don't know if my reasoning, judgment and decision making are good or sound. I do want you to know that we love you and will never turn our back on you. Should you want and ask my advice, I'll give it to you; however, I don't expect you to follow my advice blindly, for you are now a man and must follow your own route. My thought process has been prejudiced by a depression in my youth and insecurity, by a religious fanatical mother who I could not reason with, by a war in which I was in the infantry, and so forth. I find myself not wanting the world to change, but I see change, and there must be change. I also feel a little older and am reluctant to start new ways.

Please remember this from here on: Only you can control your destiny. No one else can study for you. No one else can discipline your mind; force yourself to read good literature and leave the pornography for others; only you can exercise your athletic body regularly so you feel good; only you can force yourself to think and reason honestly; only you can say no to temptation. The world will want you to roll in the gutter with them, but you will have in the long run their respect if you demand it.

I hope you develop a strong character to go along with your fine mind, handsome looks and wonderful body. From now on, only you can control your destiny. Give some thought to what you want to become & do. If your ambitions are high—go to work. I'll be around, any time you want me, I'll be there—because I care more than you'll ever know, my son.

All love, Dad

My body shook with sobs. I turned around and looked for him. I felt he was in the kitchen with me. He was sharing his most closely guarded feelings and fears. He was giving me fatherly advice as meaningful now as it was forty years ago. My father was telling me how much he loved me. I cried for several minutes, but was careful to not spill tears upon my most precious gift.

I returned to the beach, my father's letter clutched in my hand, and greeted several close friends and other family who had arrived during my absence. I shared with them the story of my summer in Coalwood, the call forty years later from Emily Buckberry, and how my father's letter was returned to me. I read a few sentences from the letter and everyone was crying after the closing lines, *I'll be around, any time you want me, I'll be there—because I care more than you'll ever know—my son. All love, Dad.* They understood the otherworldly power of his words—the incredible synchronicity of this moment. We were gathered at the beach on this November 8, 2008, to celebrate Jimmy's twenty-fifth birthday. The letter came on our son's birthday! My father knew this day would be one of the hardest days of my life and he was there for me, as he promised he would be.

I wasn't the only one to receive a long-forgotten or misplaced missive on this day of great sorrow and wonder. After our day at the beach, Brittany and Ryan went home, exhausted and emotionally drained. As Brittany curled into her favorite chair, Ryan went to the bookcase. He began running his finger along the spines, randomly pulling out a book here and there, looking for something that might offer a bit of comfort.

Suddenly he called, "Brittany! Come here!"

She ran to see what had him so excited. In his hands was a paperback copy of *Siddhartha* by Hermann Hesse, and wedged in the middle, like a bookmark, was a goofy birthday card. A wild-eyed young woman stared from the cover, accompanied by the caption "She had not yet decided whether to use her power for good... or for evil." Inside was a canned birthday wish and this handwritten message:

"Which have you decided? Of course you're beyond good and evil! I toast you to a future quarter century of passionate pursuits! (you'll never regret it). I love you eternally, Happy Birthday. Jimmy"

Jimmy had given Brittany that book and card on February 28th, 2005, in honor of her twenty-fifth birthday. Four years later, he "gave" it again, on what would have been his twenty-fifth birthday. Jimmy reminded his big sister *I love you eternally,* and my father reassured me *I'll be around, any time you want me, I'll be there.* What a day this had turned out to be. My father showed up and took care of me and Jimmy came to rescue his sister.

A week after Jimmy's birthday and the arrival of my father's letter, I tracked down the shaman, James Powell, in London and we got on the phone together. Before the call I sent an e-mail letting him know of Jimmy's death and that I wanted to ask him something about their trip to Poland. James expressed his sincere condolences and said he definitely remembered Jimmy as very charismatic and engaging but, unfortunately, not too many of the details of their conversations or the detachment ceremony. He did recall that Jimmy told him he felt the presence of his grandfather around him and that he might be taking on some of his personality traits. I told James that my father had committed suicide in 1970. James remembered that that had come up during his conversation with Jimmy.

I gave James some details about Jimmy's accident and told him the story about my summer in Coalwood in 1968, the call decades later from Emily Buckberry, and the arrival of the letter from my father on Jimmy's birthday.

"This is utterly amazing," he said as only an Englishman with a PhD from Oxford can say it, and he then offered his interpretation: "It seems very clear to me that your father is coming through to let you know there is life, or something, after death, he loves you, and love goes on. Your father is connecting with you. He probably waited a few months after Jimmy's death to let the pain subside. Emily Buckberry appears to be a conduit in this. Jimmy may, or may not, be involved. Jimmy may not be ready to come through to you. This is all very good. There's a lot of mystery; so much we don't and maybe are not supposed to know or be aware of."

He asked me if I was open to these things and I said, "Definitely."

"Good. More may be happening."

⁓⑥⑥⑥⁓

The rescue work on our family was just beginning. On the Sunday before Christmas 2008, Hilary, Brittany, and I went to Coronado, across the bay from downtown San Diego, to meet for the first time with Tarra, a well-known medium who lives and works primarily in Sedona, Arizona, but frequently comes to Southern California to meet with clients. One of Hilary's friends who had met with Tarra after her son died recommended that we take this leap into strange territory. When we made the appointment, we didn't give her our last name or any details about why we wanted a reading; she prefers it that way. Tarra has the ability to connect with those who have departed and enable them to communicate, through her, with friends and loved ones who are living in this space. As she describes it, "I tune into frequencies others can't hear." It had been six weeks since I received the call from Emily Sue Buckberry and my father's letter. I was game for anything.

We asked each other, "What do we have to lose? We can't possibly lose any more."

And so began our journey into a realm we had never imagined.

Tarra was not like anything I expected. Her hair wasn't purple, she didn't have any piercings that I could see, and there was no crystal ball or turban or flowing robes. Tarra looked like what she is, a mom in her fifties with a New York accent and an infectious laugh and wit.

We had barely sat down in the living room of a lovely home owned by one of her clients when Tarra took Hilary's hands. "I am so sorry. You've lost a child."

Hilary burst into tears.

Tarra continued. "It's Jim or Jimmy?"

"Yes," Hilary whispered.

"That explains a lot," Tarra said. "He's been showing up in my readings of other clients for the last two days. I kept wondering, 'Who is this character?'" She looked at me. "Dad, Jimmy says, 'I can't believe you showed up. This is really cool.'"

After we had figuratively picked ourselves up off the floor, Tarra asked for some of our things—jewelry, items in our pockets. I gave her my old, bulky Casio watch and a penny. She curiously fondled the watch and asked me, "Where's the watch Jimmy left for you? He wants you to wear it." I had given the Rolex Explorer to Brittany after Tom Strickler had explained its presence in Jimmy's nightstand.

Tarra looked at the penny. "You're finding pennies all the time, aren't you?"

"Yes," I said. "I found that one next to me when I was working out at the gym two days ago."

"Jimmy is leaving those for you."

I smiled.

For over an hour she brought messages from Jimmy to each of us. It was as if Jimmy were in the room, speaking to us, giving my rational mind a real tumble. Tarra/Jimmy explained his accident in detail: too many beers that night—leaving his friend's house and deciding to walk home—turned around—shit faced—the dark corner—narrow shoulder—walking too far onto the road—no time to get out of the way—the second car. He apologized profusely for being in the wrong place at the wrong time—for the suffering he caused us. "Jimmy says he's worried about the driver of the first car. He's been drinking a lot and having trouble sleeping. You need to contact him."

I muttered to myself, "That's not going to happen."

There was deep sadness, but there were also light, even funny moments, as Jimmy worked hard to let us know he was okay and in a good place. He was travelling at light speed, anywhere he wanted to go. A U2 concert in Rome, an opera in Sydney.

At one point Tarra gave us this message. "Jimmy says, 'Tell Tony I've been following Dave Koz around. Ask Tony if he knows Dave and his music.'" Tarra laughed, "Oh, Jimmy's a character. He says, 'Tell Dave I'm better than him.' Jimmy also says, 'Tupac is here. And that means anybody can get here.'"

We all were laughing at this point—and dumbfounded. Tarra went on to share with us that she's friends with Dave Koz, one of the most well-known contemporary jazz saxophone players in the world. He's been a regular on the top of the smooth jazz recording charts for years. He hosts two nationally syndicated radio shows featuring the latest in smooth jazz and is constantly on tour all over the world and even played a gig at President Obama's first inaugural ball.

So it wasn't unusual she would mention Dave. It was the reference to Tony that blew our minds. We had not mentioned one word about a Tony or an Anthony or that Jimmy played the sax. How in the hell could she know that Jimmy was a saxophone player and that he knew Anthony Ortega? Only his students and close friends called him Tony. Jimmy's put-down of Dave also made perfect sense. Jimmy was taught by an old school jazzman and he turned up his nose at the smooth jazz artists, like Dave Koz, as too commercial and "giving in to what the masses want to hear."

I once asked Jimmy, "Why don't you ever play any Kenny G or stuff like that?"

He snorted. "*That's* not jazz!"

Then the reading turned serious again. Tarra had grave concerns about Hilary. "When Jimmy died, a part of you split. A piece of you followed him. A piece of your soul went with him." She looked at Brittany and me. "This may have happened to you, too, but it's very strong with Mom here." She refocused on Hilary. "Jimmy's telling me he can't come into your dreams or make his presence known to you because he's afraid you'll embrace him and not come back. You want to be with him so deeply, and he with you, but you can't go there. Not now. Do you understand what I'm talking about?"

Hilary nodded.

"When you're asleep he sometimes sits on the bed, but he won't wake you. You aren't ready. I strongly recommend that you see Jade Wah'oo Grigori, a shaman and colleague of mine, who also lives in Sedona. We refer to Jade as the 'Big Guns.' He's Mongolian and a strange-looking dude, but he is highly experienced in these things. Call Jade and tell him about Jimmy's death and that a part of you split with him. Have Jade help you retrieve the piece of your soul that left to be with Jimmy. Jade will be coming to San Diego next month. Go see him. Tell him you need a Soul Retrieval Ceremony."

I was flabbergasted. Retrieve Hilary's soul? A Mongolian shaman? What the hell was Tarra talking about? Another shaman? Nevertheless, I decided to let Hilary make the decision. I couldn't stand to watch her slipping away into her private sorrow.

As we drove home, Hilary said, "I truly believe that Tarra's the real deal." Brittany and I agreed, but Hilary seemed sad. "What's wrong?" I asked. "When Tarra asked if we had any questions, she jumped to something else before I could ask mine. I so desperately wanted to know, 'Is he happy?'"

Six days later

Our grief couldn't hold back the calendar, and the holiday we most dreaded arrived. I woke, burdened by such a feeling of loss that I wanted to burrow under the covers and stay there. How could Hilary and I, and the rest of the family, face the absence of our son on a day that was supposed to be about joy, hope, and new beginnings? We had managed to make a feeble effort, mainly for my niece and nephew, Claire and Leo, who had flown in from Switzerland with Laura and Anton. Four and a half months before, they had been the first people at our door after the medical examiner had delivered the news of Jimmy's death. Now they had come to prop us up during an exceptionally difficult holiday.

I sighed, rolled out of bed, and got ready to face the day.

The phone rang. Hilary answered and spoke for a few minutes while I wondered who could be calling this early. She hung up, shaking her head.

"That was Tarra," she spoke with a twinkle in her eye I had not seen for a long time. "She said she usually doesn't call clients after their readings, but Jimmy has been pestering her this morning and he told Tarra she had to call 'Mom' and let her know that he's happy, and he wants all of us to celebrate today."

Hilary's question had been answered.

"Tarra also said Jimmy is definitely going to be around us today. And there may also be something happening with the phones. And, honey? Tarra said you should answer the next call."

I began to wonder if Tarra had lost it. But she'd been right about so many things during our reading that I didn't wonder for long.

My mom, Brittany, and Ryan came to our house, and around noon, after we had gone through the motions of opening a few presents, the phone rang. I reached for it. "Hello?"

"Casey, this is John Dale. Can I come over? I have something for you guys." John lives and works as a waiter, writer, actor, and radio talk show host in Los Angeles. He grew up in Solana Beach, and he and Jimmy had been good friends since the second grade. They had been roommates in L.A. for about a year and a half after graduating from college and were collaborating on several comedic writing and acting endeavors when the accident happened.

John had done so much for us since Jimmy died. He handled all of the audio-visual logistics for Jimmy's service and delivered a beautiful and, not surprisingly, funny eulogy for his pal. John's opening line brought the house down: "If this were anyone else, I would have asked Jimmy to write this for me, so I would seem a much better writer. Jimmy and I were writing partners and comedy partners since college, so forgive me if I am tempted to try to make this funny. It is our nature and I think he would have wanted me to." Pointing to Jimmy's casket on the stage, he said, "Jimmy is dressed in one of my suits, a tie from his dad, and, yes, socks that don't match."

John had visited us many times over the last few months—he was suffering greatly like the rest of us and Jimmy's friends—and he was one of only a handful who really worked to stay close and help us.

"Sure," I said. "Come on over."

"Who was that?" Hilary asked.

"John Dale," I said. "He's coming over to bring us something."

"He's pretty brave to come over on the first Christmas without his best friend," Hilary said.

The doorbell rang and I went down to answer it. John stood there, holding out a package. "I thought you might like to have this."

"Come on up," I replied and led the way to the living room. Then I tore off the wrapping. I gasped and held up a framed black-and-white photo of Jimmy playing his saxophone in front of Torrey Pines High School. The photograph captures Jimmy from his shoulders down to his knees. There's a drum kit in the background. His hands caress his instrument as he leans forward, pressing into the groove. I can sense the movement and hear the music.

"I think it was taken at one of the Battle of the Bands contests during our senior year," John said with a slight grin. "We weren't really that good. Just winged it. But we had an awesome sax player. Jimmy always thought we won, but I'm pretty we got beat out by a Metallica-wannabe band."

Jimmy played his instrument with the precision of a surgeon, yet when he got into a song his soul flew free for all to see. It takes talent and guts to let go like that, not unlike taking off your clothes before hundreds of people and saying, "Well, this is me." Jimmy could read music, but he used no props when he performed. He took the elements of whatever tune the band was playing and then explored on his own, unafraid, inquisitive, letting the music, the feel, take him. Eight years with Tony instilled in him the confidence that he wouldn't falter on his journey. No safety net required. Yet he always stayed connected with his bandmates and they remained in sync even as Jimmy explored the edges of the melodic universe. All of this and more was in the picture John had given us.

John left a short time later after another round of thanks, hugs, and a few tears. We placed the picture on the couch, then on the piano. Jimmy was with us this Christmas Day, as we so hoped he would be.

Not more than five minutes later, the phone rang and I answered, just as Tarra had instructed.

"Hi, Casey. It's John again," he stammered. "Did you just call me?" He sounded nervous.

"No," I said, puzzled.

His next question was even stranger. "Is Jimmy's cell phone still working?"

"Well, we have his phone, but the battery's dead, I'm pretty sure his number has been removed from our account for a few months now. Did he call you?"

John hesitated. "I don't know who called."

A long moment of silence. Then he said, "It was a stupid question. Sorry to have bothered you. Bye." The call ended awkwardly. I hung up and told the family, "John thinks he just got a call from Jimmy."

Brittany grabbed her cell and dialed John's number, going into the kitchen to talk to him. A few minutes later, she came back to the living room, her face pale. "Jimmy's number *did* show up on John's caller I.D. but nobody said anything when John answered. He told me he was really nervous, but he had to call back. He punched the speed dial number for Jimmy and after a couple of rings some guy answered.

"He said, 'Hi, this is John Dale. Did you just call me?'

"'Dude, why would I call you? I don't even know you.'

"'No, of course you don't. I'm sorry. Never mind.'

"He's really freaked out. I told him about Tarra and how she told us that Jimmy is going to be around and something might be happening with the phones today."

Goose bumps erupted on my arms.

Brittany continued, "So some stranger now has Jimmy's phone number. But his contacts memory wouldn't be attached to the number. What are the chances that whoever has Jimmy's number now would randomly dial John Dale's number?"

"Slim and none," I said.

Hilary was wide eyed as she replied, "Jimmy called John. Tarra said something may happen with *the* phones. She didn't say it would be *our* phone. Jimmy thanked John for bringing the photo and helping Jimmy show up for us on Christmas."

Around five that afternoon, after everyone had left, our house phone rang and once more I answered. It was Dave Koz.

"I'm so sorry to hear about Jimmy," Dave said. "I know how difficult this day must be for you all. I just wanted to let you know I'm thinking of you and send you my love and blessings. Oh, by the way, Tarra's a friend of mine and called me after your reading. She said the reading was amazing and told me all about your son's music."

I cleared my throat. "I have to tell you, during our reading Jimmy came through really strongly. He said he's been following you around, and says to tell you he's better than you. I have no idea where that comes from, unless it's because he studied with a really old-school jazzman. Jim didn't care too much for smooth jazz," I added apologetically.

Dave laughed. "No offense taken."

I thanked him for calling. "I'm utterly amazed that we're having this conversation at all. It must have taken a lot of courage and sensitivity for you to call complete strangers on Christmas, of all days."

"It was my pleasure," he said and hung up.

Wow! Was this what Tarra meant by something happening with the phones today, a call from Dave? And more food for thought. What motivates someone like Dave Koz to pick up the phone on Christmas night, as he's beginning a celebration with his family, and reach out to strangers lost in the throes of their grief for their son and brother on their first Christmas without him? Why did John Dale get a phone call from Jimmy?

Maybe it's something about saxophone players.

THE RABBIT HOLE

Alice: I can't remember things before they happen!
The White Queen: It's a poor sort of memory that only
works backwards.

Lewis Carroll, *Through the Looking-Glass*

WHEN ALICE FOLLOWED the White Rabbit into the rabbit
hole, she found a world in which the rules as we know them
don't apply. For the last year, I felt like I'd followed her. My world
shrank as if I had drunk from that bottle, closing in on me after Jimmy's
death. I wondered if it would ever expand to fullness again. Everything I'd
ever believed in seemed to have been rewritten in some strange language
that could only be deciphered by a native inhabitant of this world of pain.

On April 26, 2009, Hilary and I went to the North Coast Repertory
Theatre in Solana Beach to see the Pulitzer Prize–winning play, *Rabbit
Hole,* written by David Lindsay-Abaire. Some friends of Hilary mentioned
that we might want to see it, but that maybe we weren't ready.

As we picked up our tickets, Hilary asked how much longer the show
would be running.

The cashier said, "This is the last show. You got here just in time."

After we took our seats we looked around the small theatre. We seemed
to be the youngest people in the audience.

The play is about a family that loses a four-year-old son, Danny, and how the family members deal with the tragedy. Becca, the mother, packs up Danny's belongings, sells the house, even erases the last home video of him. Howie, her husband, retreats into depression and accuses Becca of trying to obliterate the memory of their child. Izzy, Becca's younger sister, is pregnant, and Becca mourns the loss of her child while questioning whether Izzy is fit to raise her baby. Nat, the women's mother, has experienced her own grief when her son, addicted to heroin, commits suicide.

The most influential and critical character in the drama is Jason Willette, the seventeen-year-old who struck Danny with his car eight months earlier and must live with the consequences. Danny had chased their dog into the street. Jason had no time to stop the car. Nobody's fault.

During the second act our attention was riveted on Jason. We were consumed with his pain, his torment and his suffering, his desperate need to connect. After Jimmy was killed we'd had no desire to contact the driver who hit him. Ryan had found out his name was Peter. His car had rolled but Peter had escaped unhurt, except for a few minor bumps and scrapes.

A week before we decided to see the play, a friend of mine, who knew Jimmy well, was playing golf at the club where Peter was working. Peter had been on his way to his job at the course when his car struck Jimmy that early Saturday morning. My friend's playing partner pointed out Peter and said, "That's the kid whose car struck and killed another kid a few blocks from here. He's having a really hard time."

My friend stared. "He hit Jimmy Gauntt. I knew Jimmy his whole life. His folks are good friends of ours."

Tarra's/Jimmy's words from our first reading flooded in: *He's having a hard time. Trouble sleeping. You need to contact him.*

Hilary and I were unsure. What if he didn't want to hear from us? What if his pain was too great for him to face us? Did we want to put him—and ourselves—through even more circles of hell? We procrastinated.

As the play ended, we did our best to stanch the flow of tears and control our sobs before we left the theatre with the rest of the red-eyed crowd. As we were climbing into my car, Hilary yelled.

"What happened?"

"I think a bee stung me."

I looked at her neck and saw the stinger. I pulled it out with my fingernails. "Are you allergic?"

"I don't know. I've never been stung before." She paused, a far-off look in her eyes. "I think somebody's trying to tell us something. This was the last performance of this play. Their son is killed accidently by a car driven by a young man eight months earlier. It's been eight months since Jimmy's accident. We've got to contact that boy!"

As soon as we got home, I sat down, booted up the computer, and began a letter to Peter. I introduced myself and said I was writing on behalf of my wife, Hilary, our daughter, Brittany, and Jimmy. "It is very important for you to know we are not mad or angry with you. We do not blame you for the accident. We do feel very sad and sorry that you and our son had to be on that road, at that particular place at that particular time. If we could turn back the clock and change something, anything, so you weren't there or Jimmy wasn't there, at the moment, we would do it in a heartbeat, and we know you would too. Unfortunately we don't have that power. We are truly sorry for you, truly sorry that you were the one driving that car.

"We want you to know that Jimmy is doing okay, that he's happy and he's in heaven. We also know that Jimmy wants you to know this, and he wants you to be okay, as do we. Each one of us has a full life to live, and we know Jimmy does not want this accident and his death to get in the way of us living our lives and smiling.

"We can't imagine what you have been going through. We are sorry that you've had to suffer from this. I don't know if receiving and reading this letter will be of help to you. We hope it is. You are in our thoughts and prayers, and we want and choose for you to be well."

Ryan took the letter to the golf course and asked the head pro to please deliver the letter to Peter, which he did on May 1. Ryan did a lot of the heavy lifting for us after Jimmy died. He recovered Jimmy's car from where he'd left it that Friday night, cleaned it up and sold it. Although they only knew each other for four years Jimmy and Ryan became close, like brothers. There was a very clear but unspoken rule in our family. Whenever Britt brought a new boyfriend home, Jimmy would subtly conduct a rigorous examination of physical, intellectual, and moral attributes. He never had to verbalize the results. Britt just knew when a potential boyfriend failed or passed the Jimmy Test. If he failed, she dropped him like a stone.

Ryan and Jimmy both enjoyed a passion for writing, literature, poetry, music, and the theatre. No one laughed harder than Jimmy at Ryan's jokes and impersonations. They deeply respected and admired one another. Ryan is an exceptional writer and he penned Jimmy's obituary, of which Jimmy would have been very proud. Ryan became part of our family when he married our daughter, but he won our hearts and souls with everything he did, and continues to do, after Jimmy died. He became blood.

Three months later, on July 22, my assistant, Shelley, came into my office and dropped the mail in my inbox on the credenza in back of me. I rarely get any real mail these days. All the good stuff is sent online. So, figuring it was mostly interoffice stuff, newspapers or junk, I didn't look at it right away.

I thumbed through the short stack and saw an envelope addressed to me in neat handwriting. As I looked at the name and return address in the top left corner, I froze. It was from Peter.

I closed my door, sat in my chair, and opened the letter. My hands were shaking. Before long, I was weeping. I put the letter down and cried hard for five minutes. It was powerful, it was sensitive, it was healing. The enormity of the moment and this connection was nearly overwhelming. I called Hilary and told her what had just happened, and e-mailed her a copy of the letter.

Because of our profound respect for Peter and his privacy, I will not share here the contents of Peter's letter to us, except for this one paragraph.

He wrote, "I would like to share with you a dream I had… My dream started with my getting out of my car that was on its side. I stood up and opened the passenger door to get out just like it really happened, but when I opened the door, there stood a middle-aged woman with her arms wide open with love and care, giving me help. I then turned to see Jimmy lying in the street, calm and breathing, with a middle-aged man kneeling over him, holding his hand and comforting him. You may interpret this dream any way you wish, but I felt that the woman was God assuring me that both Jimmy and I were not alone during the accident, and that the man was Jesus Christ comforting Jimmy and accepting him in his kingdom. So when you spoke of Jimmy being in a better place, I truly believe in my heart that he is and that in time we will finally meet."

That evening, Brittany came by the house and we gave her a copy of the letter. Her chin trembled as she went into another room to read it. Hilary and I went onto the deck, letting our daughter have her privacy with Peter's powerful words. A few minutes later, she joined us, her face tear streaked.

"That is so beautiful!" she said.

And for the rest of the evening, we reminisced, laughed, cried, and forgave.

―✎―

On July 28, I wrote a letter to the playwright, David Lindsey-Abaire. My intuition insisted that he had to know our story. I related how our son had died and how in *Rabbit Hole* he had captured exactly the feelings we experienced and were still experiencing. I thanked him for his gift of such a stunning work and explained how our son had been pursuing a career in writing, having completed several plays and screenplays.

I went on to say, "Grief, suffering and healing are complex and unique and personal to everyone who is touched by a loss. We can't see what's ahead of us; we do our best to control our fear and work hard to stay in the light. We commend you for being able, not having personally experienced this kind of loss (correct?), to get your arms around this subject and for your soft touch in exploring the depths of it."

I concluded, "If someone had told us a year ago we'd be writing and receiving letters like this, well, we would of course have thought we'd stumbled upon a hookah-smoking caterpillar in a rabbit hole. Thank you for kicking us over the edge into our personal rabbit hole. We are forever grateful to you. Peter is too; we're certain of it."

In August I received a reply from Lindsay-Abaire. He thanked me for my letter and offered condolences. "I can't begin to fathom the pain of your loss. The thoughts and prayers of my family are with yours."

He went on to say, "You might be interested to know that the seed of the play first came to me while I was a student at Juilliard, and a teacher posed a challenge: If you want to write a good play, think of the thing that scares you most in the world, and write about that fear. It wasn't until I became a father many years later, and I heard a few stories of children dying unexpectedly, that I was able to turn that challenge into what became *Rabbit Hole*. The mere thought of losing my son made me understand fear in a way I never had before. And so, while I had experienced death and loss, and dealt with grief to some extent, you're correct in assuming that I hadn't experienced the very specific loss that the family in the play, and your family in real life, had experienced. Which makes hearing from you that I got it right all the more special to me.

"As a writer, I hope to reach people, and to have my work connect with them in a significant way. I have no doubt that Jimmy hoped to do this in his work as well. I've been extra lucky to also receive some nice reviews, and some significant prizes. But even with all that, for as long as I've been doing this, I have never received something so humbling, and so gratifying, as the kind letter you've sent me.

"I can't tell you how moved I am to hear that *Rabbit Hole* may have played a role in you and your wife finally deciding to reach out to the young man involved in your son's accident. Thank you for including the correspondence you shared with Peter. I found it both heartbreaking and uplifting. It was clearly important and helpful for all of you to reach out to one another, and I could not be happier that you've all found a little more comfort in doing so…. It is my deep belief that through connection we heal…. Your story is a testament to that idea. It's also a testament to Jimmy and the legacy he leaves behind. He was obviously a special person who touched many lives. And by your sharing your family's story with me, I too now feel connected in some way to the light that was and continues to be Jimmy. I thank you for that. It's something I will cherish always.

All the best to you and your family,
David Lindsay-Abaire"

We received David Lindsay-Abaire's letter on August 11, 2009, two days after the first anniversary of our son's accident. That day was also Hilary's and my thirty-sixth wedding anniversary.

DOING THE WORK

ARRA SENT HILARY and me this e-mail in late September of 2009: "I am doing a workshop in Sedona and it's definitely something you should come to. We are focusing on the Ancestors and departed loved ones coming through. They are hounding me, which is why I'm getting little sleep right now."

Although each of us had seen therapists individually over the past year, we had shied away from grief groups. Hilary bonded early with three other mothers who live nearby and had all lost sons in their late teens or early twenties within six months of each other. My "fraternity" would come together later. Those conversations with moms and dads who have experienced this same hell are ones you just can't have with anyone else.

Several months earlier, for my fifty-ninth birthday, Hilary, Brittany, and I met up with Tarra's friend, Jade Wah'oo Grigori, and he led us through a Soul Retrieval Ceremony. Unfortunately, Hilary's soul had not been pieced back together as we had hoped. Obviously there was much more work to be done. I had begun to write, and my first project was to compose the extraordinary story of being reunited with the letter from my father. I shared the story with friends and family, but our grief seemed too private to share with strangers.

We had a family meeting. "So, do you want to go to Sedona?" I asked my wife and daughter. They looked at each other and nodded. Maybe we wanted to go because we knew and trusted Tarra, or maybe our grief had grown too huge to bear alone any longer.

A couple of weeks before the workshop, Tarra sent out another e-mail to us and twenty-two others to confirm the schedule and added, "This will be a life-changing and unforgettable experience, and I am very proud of all of you who've taken this leap of faith. The teachers, guides and loved ones are smiling down on each of you for hearing and answering the call and for your commitment to move ahead, through all the chaos and pain in the last few years. You are saying you are ready, really ready, to move on and to honor those that have gone on."

The idea of spending three days in a room with people we'd never met before, all of whom had suffered the loss of someone close to them, made my palms sweat. From moment to moment I waffled on canceling the trip, yet every time I tried to voice my misgivings to Hilary, the words died, only to creep back into consciousness without warning.

Apparently I wasn't the only one with reservations. One evening, as we watched television, Hilary muted the volume and took my hand. "How is Tarra going to pull this together? Is she just going to wing it?" she asked.

"Probably," I replied. At our first reading with her she jumped all over the place—talking to Jimmy, talking to us, looking into the future. She was definitely a free-flowing spirit.

Hilary, Brittany, and I arrived in Sedona on Friday, November 6th. The weather was perfect: temperatures in the high seventies, sky so blue it hurt to look at it. It was a shame we'd be stuck inside for most of the weekend, but we hadn't come to golf or play tennis, only to heal. After we got settled in our rooms at the Sunset Chateau, a cozy hotel owned by a Swiss couple, we prepared to meet the other participants. Tarra gathered all of us in the hotel lobby. As we mingled and introduced ourselves before boarding a bus for the first leg of our adventure, I sensed reluctance and discomfort from everyone. We were about to share our most private sorrows with strangers. But the question loomed in every glance. What were their stories? Was I—were we—ready to expose ourselves to the scrutiny and the sympathy of others? I tucked my hesitation inside and got ready to meet whatever was in store.

George Sanchez, a Yaqui Indian colleague of Tarra's, took us "walking the land." Towering red cliffs seemed to pierce the sky, making me feel very small and insignificant. Sun warmed the earth and a few wispy clouds drifted over the cliffs. Creosote and cactus dotted the landscape.

George's face seemed to have been carved by a harsh sun and harsher life. I guessed he was in his early sixties; his eyes held a depth of experience and understanding that made him seem ageless. He played the flute and a drum as we walked the packed red earth. He spoke seldom, but we gleaned a story of too many years spent behind bars as a young man, an adult son who died homeless on the streets of San Diego. His life had led him to help young men battle their demons of anger and substance abuse, battles he himself had fought for years. He spoke of love. "Love is everything. Love everybody." My nervousness about what we would undergo this weekend eased. By the end of the walk, I had realigned with our purpose for being here.

For dinner, our little band shared a picnic in a nearby park. A spectacular sunset turned the sky crimson, orange, lavender, and apricot, magnificently outshining the lackluster cold sandwiches and sodas. It seemed as if God were telling us that we, too, would learn to shine through our sorrow.

On Saturday we all gathered in the meeting room of the chateau. Through large windows, we could see the mountains, framed by cedar and juniper. Colorful Indian rugs and paintings hung on the walls.

At nine o'clock, Tarra called the meeting to order. "Death is an illusion," she announced. "Our loved ones are always around us, always available to us when we open to their presence. Today you will have the opportunity to open to your loved ones, to heal the grief that has held you captive. Let's begin."

As Tarra laid out the scenarios for skits and role playing, I felt like I'd stepped into a college psychology class. Would pretending to be someone who had passed on really make a difference? As they say in betting circles, we'd paid our money and now we'd have to take our chances.

Tarra began putting participants together, in pairs or small groups. She seemed to be orchestrating events on the fly with no discernible plan.

My skepticism bloomed but the room's energy shifted into high gear, its volume and volatility astonishing.

She paired me with Jessica, a young nurse from Phoenix who had lost her father when she was thirteen. "Casey, you are Jessica's father. Jessica, now is your chance to tell your father what you never got a chance to say to him," Tarra instructed.

I felt like I'd been sucker punched. Tarra had no way of knowing that my sister, Laura, was thirteen years old when our father killed himself. Through the years I watched her struggle and suffer because of his death. In her mid-twenties, she became a nurse. Another coincidence? How would this scenario play out? Would I be able to heal my pain around Laura's, too?

Jessica and I faced each other. We breathed deeply, in and out, hoping to release our tension. She seemed tight and nervous as she began. "I hate you! I hate you! How could you leave me like that?" she screamed at her father/me. "How could you leave Mom alone to raise us by herself? How could you?" All her anger, guilt, and regret poured out in a raging cascade of tortured tears.

Sorrow overwhelmed me. Instinctively, I wrapped my arms around her and whispered, "I'm sorry. I love you," over and over as she railed and cried out her anguish. Her weeping slackened. Words flowed from me, words from the letter that my father had written to me all those years ago. "I'll be around, anytime you want me, I'll be there, because I care for you more than you will ever know." And I added some words of my own: "Don't hate me. Love me, as I do you. I never left you. I'm here." I wept as though I were weeping for not only Jessica, but for myself, my sister, my father, my son, my family, the world.

When I held Jessica as her father, I was both her father and mine. My words were from both our fathers. And I was also a brother, holding Laura, comforting the little girl who had lost her favorite person in the whole world on December 22, 1970. I held Laura/Jessica tightly, letting our anger over what our fathers had done to us, and taken from us, spill out in tears.

Tarra put on some music. "Now you can have the dance you never could have with your father on your wedding day."

"But I'm not married. Not even dating," Jessica whispered as she put her hand in mine.

"It doesn't matter," I whispered back as I took her in my arms. As we moved across the floor, I danced not only with her but with Laura, sharing the father-daughter dance that neither of them had had a chance to have. We danced to heal, danced to rejoice in a moment we thought could never come.

As the music ended, Jessica murmured, "If my dad had lived, he would be about your age. Thank you from both of us."

No one knew of the multiple layers of connection between Jessica and I, not even Hilary, until I explained it to her later that night. How had Tarra made this perfect pairing, this healing of two people who had never met before? But she was just warming up.

During introductions the day before, we had met Stephen from Boulder, Colorado. He was in his thirties, and a friend of Tarra's. "She thought I was in Prague, so she didn't tell me she was presenting this workshop," he said. "A week ago I had a strong urge to e-mail her that I was back in Boulder. Didn't take long for her to call and tell me I'd better get here right away, that I needed to be here." He grinned. "Not that she needed me, but that I needed to come. I still haven't figured out why."

That afternoon the mystery was solved. After a break, we came back to the room to find Stephen lying on the couch with a blanket over him, only his head exposed, his eyes closed. At first I thought he must be napping. Then I saw Jessica in her nurse's uniform standing next to him. Was this part of another skit?

Tarra went up to Carol, a teacher from San Francisco. When we had introduced ourselves to Carol on Friday night, she was shaking and her raw emotions were evident in her face and body. Pain oozed from her. A year ago, her son, Jeffrey, a young doctor, had accidentally taken a combination of Advil and some other medication and lapsed into a coma. For days, the family prayed for his recovery as he was fed through a tube, hydrated through a tube, living only through tubes. He lived for ten days after the family decided to remove his artificial lifelines.

Her husband and another son had elected not to join her at the workshop, leaving her to face her demons alone.

"Please go sit next to him," Tarra said. "Jeffrey is waiting."

Carol stood and walked to "Jeffrey" as if she were treading on broken glass with bare feet. Images of the movie, *Dead Man Walking*, flickered through my memory. She looked shattered, as if this would be her last walk on Earth.

Sitting on the chair next to Stephen, she began to talk. "Jeffrey, where are you? Where did you go?" Tears streaked her face as she said, "I'm so sorry, honey. We didn't want to let you go. We didn't want to take you off life support, but we had no choice. Please understand that we couldn't let you survive as a vegetable."

A thrill washed over me as Stephen opened his eyes and looked into hers. "I love you, Mom. It's okay. Let me go."

Carol stroked his face, tentatively at first, then with a tenderness that only a mother can feel. Her recovery had begun. As she left Stephen's side, a collective sigh of relief filled the room.

It was our turn. Tarra said, "Casey, would you and Hilary and Brittany come up here?"

As we approached, I stopped in my tracks as it dawned on me that Tarra had somehow recreated the scene of our visit to the medical examiner's office in those first hours after Jimmy's death: the three of us huddled together looking through the glass at Jimmy's body as it lay on the gurney, the blanket pulled up to his chin. Every detail the same—except one. Stephen lay in the opposite direction that Jimmy had lain in the morgue. The apparent contradiction felt right; we would see the undamaged side of our son's face.

Weeping with sorrow, we gathered beside him. This time no pane of glass separated us. I touched his hair. "Goodbye, son," I murmured.

Brittany stroked his cheek, whispering her farewell.

Hilary, oblivious to the tears that fell onto Stephen's skin, leaned over and kissed "Jimmy's" lips, the way she always had whenever he left, even to go to a music lesson or the arcade. It was the only way she knew how to say goodbye. "I love you, my precious prince," she whispered.

Stephen/Jimmy lay with eyes still closed, not speaking. Tears spilled from his eyes as we touched and stroked our son as we talked to him. We were finally getting the chance to do what we'd been denied at the M.E.'s office sixty-four Saturdays ago.

Later I asked Tarra, "How did you know to position Stephen so that his 'good' side was facing us?"

She replied, "Stephen was originally facing the other way. I repositioned him before you came into the room. I wasn't sure why then, but I am now. The teachers that guide me wanted you to see 'Jimmy's' undamaged side. I always trust Spirit."

Brittany, three months pregnant, was next in line for Tarra's healing work. Brittany's epilepsy didn't stop her and Ryan from trying to start a family, but she was worried. Hilary had miscarried once before Brittany came into this world, and our anxiety around our daughter's pregnancy was great.

Tarra helped Brittany strap on a false belly to simulate being nine months pregnant. Brittany lay down on the couch and, with Jessica in her nurse's role, acted out giving birth to a healthy baby.

Brittany had a complete meltdown, sobbing and stuttering out her fears. Ever since Jimmy had passed away, she had felt tremendous pressure to make Hilary and me happy. "I'm so afraid I'll let you down, especially if I don't deliver a healthy baby," she cried.

Hilary and I enfolded her in a shared embrace. "Oh, honey," Hilary assured her through her own tears, "you aren't responsible for our feelings. Our grief isn't your stone to carry."

"Please don't worry about us," I chimed in. "We love you. Your love is all that matters."

As she wept in our arms, her energy shifted, and we knew that her fear was receding.

After hours of rampant emotions, after every participant had had a chance to share in the magic of the day, we took a break. I felt like I had been run over by a Mack truck. I had cried more than half of the past eight hours, yet I had never felt so connected to so many people.

When we reassembled, Tarra asked us all to lie down on the floor. "We're going to do a guided meditation to connect with our spirit guides and those on the other side," she explained. "So get comfortable and close your eyes. Take a deep breath, hold it, exhale. Relax your minds and bodies."

My eyes closed and my muscles seemed to melt into the carpet as I breathed deeply and rhythmically. Beside me I could hear Hilary's breathing beginning to match mine. I had no trouble relaxing; I was rag-limp. The stress of the last fifteen months had been carried away on a river of tears.

After a few minutes, Tarra began to speak, softly and slowly. "You are standing before a gate that opens into a beautiful garden. You step through the gate. In front of you grows a solitary red rose. Observe the rose, its perfection. Breathe deeply of its scent."

Looking into the heart of the imaginary rose, I leaned over and inhaled its sweet odor.

Tarra's voice lulled us. "There is a small stream with a bridge over it. Slowly cross the bridge, watching the sunlight sparkle on the water, hearing the gurgle as the stream flows gently over small stones. As you step off the bridge on the other side, you will meet your guide, or guides, who will take you to a crowd of people. You may know some of the people, or you may not."

Again, I followed her directions. I walked over the stream and saw... nothing. No guide, no crowd. All I saw was a turquoise palette of light, the same colors I had seen during our Soul Retrieval Ceremony with Shaman Jade Wah'oo. I tried to look through the color, to find someone or something. Still nothing. I retraced my steps into the garden, then turned around and went back over the bridge. Same thing: turquoise light, nobody there. Suddenly flash images of several unknown faces appeared, one at a time, flying into view and quickly vanishing.

Tarra's voice brought me out of my trance. Disappointment perched on my shoulder, whispering that somehow I had failed, as I listened to others in the group describe their meetings.

Brittany's turn came. "At first I didn't see anyone, no guide, no crowd. I was discouraged so I turned to go back. Standing next to the bridge was a tall, handsome, blond young man. He wore a white linen shirt and slacks. Gold necklaces and bands hung around his neck. Not bling. Something very elegant. He took my hand and helped me over the bridge and then he was gone. I know he was my guide."

Hilary's experience was similar to mine. "I've done similar guided meditations many, many times," she said. "Jimmy and others have frequently come to me, but not this time." She looked forlorn. I took her hand in silent sympathy.

That evening George invited us to his small rented house in nearby Cottonwood for a "baby sweat." I had never been to a sweat lodge before and was leery at first. A month earlier in Sedona, not too far from where we were, two people had died participating in a group sweat lodge led by a well-known self-help guru. The national media splashed the story across page and screen. I could see my doubt echoed in the eyes of the others. Would this help or harm us?

Several yards away from a large, twenty-foot-tall tepee, a low-slung tent that seemed to have been cobbled together with tarps and blankets crouched next to a fire that burned brightly. Hummingbird, George's wife, approached Brittany. "Sweats are not good for pregnant women. You come with me," she said, leading Brittany and several others who were not up for the sweat to the tepee. The rest of us followed George to the "lodge."

"Take off as much clothing as you are comfortable shedding," he instructed as he began undressing. "The more, the better."

Feeling awkward and shy, I stripped down to my boxers, avoiding looking at the others. George held aside the flap that covered the entrance to the low structure and we entered one by one, arranging ourselves against the canvas walls, circling the red-hot rocks that had been carried in on a shovel from the fire outside. Before I managed to sit cross-legged on the far side of the tent, sweat was pouring from me. I don't know why I was so bashful. It was pitch-black inside the tent. Other than a faint glow from the rocks, I couldn't see anything. Hilary was next to me and she stripped off everything but her panties. George sang a prayer and tossed some sage on the rocks. The strong, sweet smoke filled the tent, its leaves bursting into tiny sparks dancing up into the blackness.

George invited each of us to share our intentions of why we had come. One by one we spoke our heavy truths, punctuated by more sage tossed on the rocks and George's soft words: "That's so beautiful. I love you." Fifteen of us huddled semi-naked and sweating, shoulder to shoulder as we bared our souls and shared our loads. Our suffering and pain poured from us along with the sweat, cooled only slightly by our tears. Mary, one of our compatriots, took a photo of some us as we emerged from the lodge. She gasped and rushed over to show us the results. Above our heads were hundreds of tiny orbs of bluish-white light. We were not alone.

On Sunday we had a closing celebration lunch. Tarra brought a birthday cake and we all sang happy birthday to Dr. Robert Cherney, one of the participants, and to Jimmy Gauntt for his twenty-sixth birthday. We hugged each other warmly as we said our goodbyes. We were no longer strangers, and it was somehow clear that we never had been.

That evening, back in Solana Beach, Hilary and I went to bed, exhausted from the emotional roller coaster we'd been on for two days. One of Tarra's healers had given us a parting gift of scented healing water. Hilary spritzed some on our pillows, and soothed by the smell, we drifted off quickly.

Early the next morning, I dreamed. I was aware that I was dreaming but was very close to waking. I believe it's called lucid dreaming. After Jimmy's passing I began keeping a journal, and I try to write down these dreams right after I wake up. Some of the dreams are so elusive that when I go back and read them in my journal I have no memory of ever having them or writing them down. The journal is my "dream catcher."

In this dream Indian George appeared wearing a worn, beige, long-sleeved shirt and a headband. "Come. Follow me," he said. We walked into a large, comfortable living room in a house, or maybe a hotel lobby, where a group of people seated on couches and easy chairs chatted. My mother was among them. In mid-conversation she looked up and smiled at me, unsurprised to see me. She looked thirty years younger than her age of eighty-eight at the time of the dream. Her red lipstick brightened her face. Strangely, her ever-present cigarette was missing. I could hardly remember a time when she wasn't holding one. Without uttering a word to me, she turned back to her conversation, and I followed George outside.

Warm sun and pine trees surrounded us. We seemed to be at a mountain campsite. Someone sat at a crude table, a slab of wood placed on a tree stump. A cold fire pit was nearby. I didn't recognize the man at first; a bright glow surrounded him.

Then, without seeing his face, I knew it was Jimmy. I felt him. He was so familiar. "Hi, Dad," he said. "I love you."

"I love you too, son," I replied. "Is there any message you want me to take back with me?"

"Tell Britt and Mom that I love them. I'm so happy you went to Sedona. Make sure Mom keeps doing the work. It's helping her, but she needs to continue it and get better. Help her."

George touched my arm and I knew it was time to go. As we went down the hill, the air seemed to shimmer in front of us, as if seen through a pane of super-thin glass. George stepped through, me close behind. Suddenly I was flying, close to the ground. My belly scraped the tall grass, and I remembered how I love to fly. And then I woke, eager to deliver Jimmy's messages.

My spirit guide had shown up. George had been with me the entire weekend.

THE COFFEE READER

━━━

I T HAD BEEN three months since our trip to Sedona, yet our work was not finished. The work is never finished.

Hilary and I sat in the conference room of the Solana Beach Marriott Courtyard hotel. We'd just finished one of Tarra's weekend psychic workshops and were waiting to see Mary, The Coffee Reader. I'd dabbled in reading tea leaves, making up "fortunes" for the kids whenever we'd go out for Chinese food, but coffee reading? Our hearts and minds had been greatly softened and expanded in Sedona and we were at the point of "bring it on." Coffee reading is an ancient art that originated in the Middle East. It involves interpreting the coffee grounds that remain in a cup of strong Turkish coffee. Mary emigrated from Iran and now she and her granddaughter were taking workshop participants to the next level of awareness.

Mary's granddaughter brought Hilary and me each a cup of thick, black brew that smelled much stronger than the Starbucks and fresh-ground coffee we ordinarily drank. "Drink most of it," she instructed as she handed us the cups and saucers, "but leave a little. Then cover the cup with the saucer and turn it over. Hold them tightly together for a minute or so. Then I will be back to take them to my grandmother."

We did as she asked, choking slightly at the coffee's strength and taste. Carefully, we turned our cups over and held them until the granddaughter returned. "I will come back for you when Grandmother finishes with the reading she's doing now." We handed her our cups and saucers and waited.

Soon the granddaughter returned and escorted us to a hotel room down the hall. Then she went to stand beside Mary, who was seated at a table. The Coffee Reader seemed to be about seventy years old, well dressed, with impeccably groomed, thick, coal black hair, and wearing lots of gold jewelry. "Please, sit," she said, pointing to the two chairs across the table from them. Both women seemed to be agitated or excited. We weren't sure which.

The cups sat side by side, still upside down on their saucers. Mary pointed to the saucer to her left. "Who belong to this?"

Damn! It hadn't occurred to me to mark my cup. I had no idea which was mine.

"It's mine," Hilary said firmly.

Mary grabbed the bottom of Hilary's cup and lifted it. The saucer stuck to the cup's rim. "This very rare!" she exclaimed.

The granddaughter chimed in. "It has happened only a couple of times in the thirty-five years my grandmother has been doing this."

Mary's dark eyes drilled into Hilary's. "You will get everything you wish for this year. This is the sign of good luck—and a good heart. You are very wise. It is all good."

Then she turned to me. "What you do? Engineer?"

I shook my head. "I'm a lawyer."

Mary gave me a withering look. "You listen to this woman. You don't know everything. She does. She is to be listened to."

And that was the end of Hilary's reading. It had lasted ninety seconds, tops. My wife had won the lottery of the coffee readings. She had hit it out of the park. Nothing more to be said.

Mary picked up my cup. The saucer remained fixed to the table as if it had been epoxied there. A small puddle of thick coffee pooled in it. Mary lifted the saucer, poured the coffee dregs onto a white napkin and looked into the cup. Time seemed to stretch as she studied the remains. Mary's English was poor, which is why her granddaughter accompanies her at these readings. Several times during my reading she and her granddaughter conferred in Persian, and the younger woman translated into English. If Mary didn't concur with the translation, they would argue in Persian until Mary was satisfied. "Something bad will happen on your job, but you will get past it. It will be okay. There's a big problem, some big case with two big firms. Something with this job is making you upset or angry. Don't finish it if it's making you upset. Walk away.

"You will make good money this year. There are three things involving money. One is your house. Three things. That's good. Three is a lucky number.

"There's a man. Maybe he is client. Be patient. He will want to argue with you. You are honest and people like and believe in you. You do excellent job.

"You have two children, yes? Everything is good there. You and your wife will have a long life together. There's a ghost in your house, but nothing to be afraid of."

What? Hilary was staring at Mary as if she couldn't believe what the woman had just said.

Mary went on. "You and your wife will go on a long holiday, but not more than two weeks. Don't go for more than two weeks. Do you have any questions?"

Hilary, near tears, didn't hesitate. "We don't have two children and everything is not good. Eighteen months ago we lost our twenty-four-year-old son."

Mary gasped as if Hilary had punched her in the stomach. "How did he die?"

Hilary told her.

Mary was silent, reflecting. Then she said in a hoarse whisper, "God gives and God takes. This can't be explained. Your son is the ghost in your house. Don't be afraid."

Tears ran down Hilary's face. "We know this and welcome his presence."

Mary's face was stern as she said, "Don't worry. Nothing bad is coming your way. Only good things."

We stood and thanked her and her granddaughter. Mary took our hands and said, "You'll be okay. It will be all right."

The "bad thing at work" began two days after our reading with Mary. My largest client, who liked to yell and scream, ran a billion-dollar investment fund. He was embroiled in a major dispute with his largest investor and one of the biggest pension funds in the world. I told him he either had to calm down or I was going to quit. He did and, although the negotiations were really tough and took place over two and a half years, everything was finally resolved in late 2012. And then I quit the law practice.

In October Hilary and I travelled to Switzerland and flew together with my sister Laura and her family to Tanzania for a photo safari and one of the best trips of our lives. We spread some of Jimmy's ashes in the low hills above the Mara River in the western Serengeti. Two weeks later we were back home.

We will always have two children. And as for our ghost? Jimmy continued to stay very busy.

THE GHOST WRITER

TO CELEBRATE MY sixtieth birthday, Hilary and I travelled with our good friends Frank and Penny Dudek to Death Valley for a weekend. We stayed at the Furnace Creek Inn, which nestles up against the Funeral Mountains. Cheery. My parents had honeymooned at the Inn in March of 1946, but none of us had been there before.

Let me back up a minute. "Good friends" is a woefully inadequate description of the Dudeks. We've known Penny and Frank since Brittany and their daughter Elizabeth were four years old. As I mentioned before, their son John was like a big brother to Jimmy—and saved his butt in the seventh grade—and their youngest, Anne, is a daughter to us. The Dudeks are family and when we lost our son, they too lost a son. They picked us up and cared for us like no one else. During that first horrible year, they had us over for dinner every Saturday night for more than just a meal: We talked, we grieved, we cried. They climbed down and walked with us in the valley of death. So it was not unusual that we would travel to Death Valley together. We'd already been there.

In spite of its name, Death Valley is really quite picturesque. In mid-January, snow capped the distant Panamint Mountains, and we hiked the slot canyons in the Funerals, marveling at the colors created by the minerals in the rock and the holes and scars of abandoned borax mines. A strangely beautiful and inspiring place, put in perspective by vestiges of toil all around, that predominantly fruitless labor of men who worked their meager claims over a hundred years ago, their remnants palpable. I thought of my parents eyeing the same scenes some sixty-five years prior. I took a few snapshots with a disposable camera I'd grabbed from the kitchen drawer.

When we returned to Solana Beach, I began to focus on the film project I'd been working on with Steve Date, a fifth-grade teacher from Minneapolis we had met at the October Sky Festival the previous fall. The annual event celebrates the fame brought to Coalwood, thanks to their favorite son, Homer "Sonny" Hickam. Hilary and I had travelled to Coalwood to personally thank Emily Sue Buckberry for keeping my dad's letter safe and getting it to me when she did. I also wanted to revisit this little town that had mysteriously come back into my life. Our introduction to Steve was serendipitous. An amateur filmmaker, he had recently completed a documentary, *Welcome To Coalwood*. Em Sue made me tell Steve a quick version of the saga of The Letter.

Steve was deeply moved. "I have my camera. Would you be okay with my filming you while you tell your story?" Ten minutes, one take. A rough cut of the film was close to being finished, and Steve had put me to work finding still photos and home movies of our family that could be spliced in. "I really want photos and pictures of objects that represent Jimmy and your father," he instructed. I had spent hours in our attic poring through photo albums and grocery bags of pictures that hadn't quite made it into albums, pulling several to send to Steve.

The next morning before heading to work, I artfully arranged on our coffee table the hard copies of Jimmy's screenplays and plays, including *The Leather Clad Chaperone* and *Now's The Time*, and snapped a few more pictures with the same camera I'd taken to Death Valley.

"What about his saxophone?" Hilary asked as she watched me work.

Of course! Henri! I pulled the much-travelled instrument out of its case, placed it on a maroon leather desk chair I dragged out on our front lawn, and photographed that. I was on a roll now.

When I got to work the next day, I took several photos of the display case on the wall behind my desk. The recently completed, professionally assembled work of art contains my dad's Legion of Merit and Bronze Star with Cluster medals and photos of my father as a soldier in his twenties. Shortly after I received the letter from my father, my mom gave me those medals, together with the orders of commendation, and Colonel Windom's journals of the actions of the 145th Infantry Division in the South Pacific that she had safeguarded all these years. She also gave me a history of Dad's regiment that he helped write as a battalion commander.

People come into my office and their eyes are drawn to the case. When they ask me, "Who is that?" I proudly tell them, "That's my father, Grover Gauntt, a distinguished Army officer during World War II." I used up the last few shots on the disposable camera. I hoped at least some of the shots of Jimmy's scripts and sax, and my dad's medals, would be good enough to send to Steve.

When I got home that evening I put the camera on Hilary's desk in our kitchen. An hour or so later I was looking for something in the junk drawer in our kitchen and spotted an older, used-up disposable camera and put that on Hilary's desk as well.

On Wednesday Hilary took both cameras to CVS to have the pictures developed.

Around two p.m. on Thursday, I got an e-mail from Hilary.

"Subject: A bit of a shock... I just picked up the photos. There he was. Two of Jimmy in his favorite spot on the couch, wrapped in the blanket with Princess on his outstretched legs. Wearing a cap and a huge grin, snacks on the table and reading a book by Phillip Roth called *The Ghost Writer,* of all things! He couldn't look happier. It seems more impossible than ever that he's gone."

I called Hilary right away.

Her voice trembled as she said, "I was just so surprised. I wasn't expecting to find a new picture of Jimmy. It was so out of the blue and so him."

That evening we looked through the snapshots from the older disposable. Pictures of our trip to Prague with the Dudeks in October 2007 and some shots taken when Hilary and I went to Borrego Springs in January 2008 bracketed the two photographs of Jimmy.

"Look how he holds the book," Hilary said, running her finger over the photo. "It's like he's deliberately showing off what he's reading." From his spot on the couch, Jimmy holds *The Ghost Writer* well out in front of him, the title and author's name clearly displayed.

"Did you take those photos?" I asked Hilary.

"I have no idea. I must have," she replied.

Memories overwhelmed me. That Friday, Jimmy's last day, was burned into my mind. When we got back to the house after our dinner at Fidel's with my sister and her family, Jimmy was in his spot, watching the opening ceremonies of the Summer Olympics in Beijing. Even though years have passed, that's still Jimmy's spot. These days when Hilary and I are in the family room talking about or to Jimmy, as we often do, we always look over to him, to his spot on the couch, and we acknowledge him. Always. Sometimes we catch each other stealing glances to see if there might be a slight depression in the cushions where his head and shoulders have pressed against them.

The past few days before Hilary picked up the packet of photos had been "heavy Jimmy days," as we call them. Memories laced with tears had followed us as we'd looked at so many pictures of him as a baby, family pictures with the four of us, birthdays, holidays, graduations, other achievements, happy times, trying to find just the right ones for Steve and the film.

These two pictures captured the things we had completely overlooked: his (never our) precious cat, Princess; a book (he was always with a book in his hand); his favorite blanket wrapped around his legs; drink glasses and snacks surrounding him; and, of course, his spot on the couch. These define Jimmy. They *are* Jimmy.

When I got Hilary's e-mail, I replied, "I think it was a present for you. He's happy. He wanted to reassure you." That was surely part of it. But I also couldn't help thinking he knew what we were up to and decided to provide some much-needed input of his own in response to Steve's request. It was as if he were telling us, "Hey, guys. Don't forget about these things!" I fired the photos off to Steve and shared with him the story of our discovery.

A few weeks after our coffee reading with Mary and the photos turning up, Hilary, Brittany, and I went to see the latest Roman Polanski film, *The*

Ghost Writer, which is completely unrelated to Roth's book. Laura had called from Switzerland that morning. I mentioned we were going to see the movie.

"Anton and I saw that last week. It's a very good film but I need to give you a heads-up. The ending is very powerful and.... Well, I don't want to say anything more about it. Just be ready," she warned.

Huge understatement, as we would find out in a few hours.

Polanski and Robert Harris, a best-selling English novelist, co-wrote the screenplay based on Harris's novel, *The Ghost*, published in September 2007. Ewan McGregor plays a writer who has been hired to ghostwrite the autobiography of the recently retired British prime minister, played by Pierce Brosnan. As he delves into the prime minister's past, he uncovers an espionage conspiracy intended by powerful people in the US and UK to remain deeply buried.

The penultimate scene of the film takes place in Manhattan at a star-studded event celebrating the release of the new book. McGregor passes a note to the widow of the recently assassinated former prime minister. She has secretly been a CIA operative during their entire marriage, and Ewan has just let her know he has put together all of the pieces of this well-crafted deception. She's on her cell phone with a co-conspirator as she watches him leave the party, the original manuscript tucked under his arm.

Chill rain soaks the streets of New York as he steps into the deserted street. As McGregor walks out of the frame to the right, the camera holds on a dark, sleek sedan, its headlights off. It roars down the street from the left, across the frame. The camera does not follow it. As we watch the rain fall on an again-deserted street, we hear a loud thump. Brakes screech. The throaty roar as the sedan accelerates. Seconds of silence. Then a rustle, like large dry maple leaves scraping the pavement. And then pages from McGregor's manuscript blow across the frame. The camera follows. They cartwheel down the street, propelled by a freshening wind.

We sat rigid in our seats, time suspended. I clutched Hilary's thigh as I said, "Brittany, are you all right?"

She stared straight as tears erupted.

I looked at Hilary. She was as frozen as our daughter, weeping quietly.

As the credits rolled, I was transported back to the last time the four of us were together. Jimmy had brought us the latest draft of *Now's The Time* and had put it on the piano bench in our family room. He could hardly wait for us to read it and talk with him about it.

His other plays and screenplays were tucked in a drawer in our bedroom. Among them was another project he had been furiously working on the last nine months of his life, a screenplay he and his friend, Evan, had ghostwritten for a major Hollywood director.

His fateful trek along Del Dios Highway. Pages of his manuscripts dancing down the dark road.

Later that evening, as Hilary and I debriefed the film experience over a glass of wine, we looked over to his spot on the couch, raised our glasses and toasted, once again, our ghostwriter.

WANT TO GO FOR A RIDE?

I N THE 1997 movie, *Contact*, a reclusive billionaire played by John Hurt takes up residence inside the Mir space station, believing that zero gravity will slow the growth of his cancer cells. On a video conference call to Jodie Foster, in which he reveals he's secretly financed the construction of a space/time travel machine, he asks her, "So, do you want to go for a ride?" She has been chosen as the emissary of the world to embark on a one-shot intergalactic, interdimensional mission to the unknown. After careening through multiple worm holes she finds herself in the most strange and beautiful place imaginable, and poses the age-old questions to a being that, for her peace of mind, has assumed the likeness of her long-dead father: "Why? Where? What is the meaning of life?"

My journey is eerily similar. Jimmy's sudden, tragic death somehow dropped me into my own worm hole, or rabbit hole. Emily Sue Buckberry was the unsuspecting lightning rod that reconnected me with my father across time and space. If that's all I ever got on my journey—reconciliation with my father—I could not have asked for more. But my ride was only getting started.

Over the years, like most people, I routinely deleted e-mails from Classmates.com urging me to sign up and see who was looking for me or to entice me to make contact with people from my alma mater, Lake Park High School in Roselle, Illinois. I hadn't kept in touch with anyone from my class of 1968 since my family and I ran out of Itasca after my dad's suicide. I didn't see any reason to reconnect with any of them forty years later.

Anyone, that is, except George Blystone, and that connection had lapsed more than two decades ago. In August 2009 I got another Classmates e-mail and reached for the delete button, but something made me hesitate. It had been almost a year since Jimmy's death and I'd been thinking about George for some reason.

George was a star athlete and the funniest guy in school. He, too, had lost his father at an early age. I always felt there was a unique bond between us. So I opened the e-mail and went to the website's message center. There were no messages for me, but I was prompted to leave a message for a classmate. On impulse, I typed, "George Blystone, where are you? Casey Gauntt," and hit the Send button.

Over the next several days I was bombarded by messages, urging me to become a paying member of Classmates.com, enticing me with messages from classmates who wanted to connect only if I would join. I was offered a "free" seven-day trial membership. I checked every day but still no messages. I noted on my calendar to cancel the trial before my credit card was nicked for the rollover one-year membership, and since I'd gotten no messages, canceled at the end of the last day. I gave up searching for George.

But Classmates.com didn't give up on me. Supposedly more and more classmates had left messages; I could find out which ones by simply signing up. So in February 2010 I gave it one more shot. Lo and behold, there were two messages for me, one dated January 19, 2010, from George Blystone: "Hey, where's the hundred dollars I loaned you for that hooker 25 years ago?"

I roared with laughter. There had been no hooker and it was twenty-two years ago, not twenty-five. In 1988, George and a buddy had come to San Diego for Super Bowl XXII, in which the Washington Redskins trounced the Denver Broncos 42-10. During dinner at the hotel where George was staying, Hilary, young Brittany and Jimmy, and I discovered that George was in advertising on the East Coast. We enjoyed a fireworks show, Jimmy ended up with a Redskins cap, and George and his friend went off to find the parties. That was the last I saw of my old friend.

Now George was back. I fired off a smart-alec reply: "Invested the $100 in a start-up with the strange name of Google. Where are you? Here's my e-mail address."

The next day at the office I received an e-mail. The subject line read: "Can you have sex after 60 without chemicals?" Vintage Blystone for sure. So was the text. "Since I'm not a member of Classmates, I just saw your message acknowledging that you took the money I gave you for a sex change operation and put it to good use. I hope that you are in good health and that mentally remaining a man was not too difficult for you. Here's my contact info. Get back to me and let me know how the Gauntt family is doing. Am off to Chicago. George."

LOL! "Thank you, Classmates.com!" I shouted. I clicked on the link to the website for George's company, Newday, a marketing firm in Connecticut. Under the "Our People" tab, I found a current picture of a balding old man with a Cheshire cat grin. I would have recognized him anywhere.

How to break the news of Jimmy's death? Not by phone. I didn't want to put George in the position of delivering a few wisecracks to break the ice, only to find out about Jimmy. I took the road less painful and e-mailed George on Monday, attaching the story of The Letter. "Good to hear from you. I checked your company's site. Jesus Christ! What happened to you? You look like you're fifty years old! I'm going to call you but I want you to read the attachment first. WARNING: Do not read this at work. And maybe have a scotch first."

I went on to tell George about Brittany and her husband, the approaching arrival of a grandchild, and other generic catch-up news. I continued, "There isn't one person from high school except you that I kept in touch with. Time has no relevance as to certain things, as confirmed by the attached story. Let me know when you've read it, gotten your breath back, and then we'll talk. Hilary says hi."

I didn't hear from George for several days and worried that breaking the news about Jimmy might have knocked him back on his heels and he didn't know what to say.

On Friday, I dialed George on his cell. When he answered, I said, "Either you forgot how to read or you need some help with the big words, so I thought I'd better give you a call."

George sounded shaken. "Oh, man. I need to talk to you, but I'm just finishing up a meeting. Can I call you back in a few?"

"Sure."

When he did, George said he was in Chicago at a business meeting with Jerry Hasseldorf, another high school classmate of ours. "I saw your e-mail before I left the office for the airport. I opened the attachment without scotch or privacy and read it. I'm so embarrassed by those idiotic e-mails I sent you. I knew about your dad and how hard that was for you. I was there with you that Christmas, remember? And when I read about Jimmy—Casey, I'm so sorry. I don't even know what to say. It's unthinkable, unimaginable."

There was silence on the line for a moment. Then he went on. "When I got to the part about the woman from West Virginia and the letter from your dad, the hair stood up on the back of my neck. When I read that it had arrived on your son's birthday, I bawled my eyes out." He took a deep breath. "I'm really shaken up by all this. It's like my beliefs are turned upside down. Not religion but, you know, what's next? What happens?"

For twenty minutes we talked about family and friends, cutting through the years of absence as only friends can do, promising to talk again in a couple of weeks.

Four days later, I got a call from Dennis Kim. Dennis and Jimmy had met at USC and had become very good friends. Dennis attended the prestigious film school there, while Jimmy was majoring in English and Spanish but spending most of his time writing plays and screenplays. Dennis had grown up in Chicago, and Jimmy had spent a long weekend there with him and his family. After graduation, Dennis went into the film business in L.A. They remained close. Jimmy and he pitched each other with an avalanche of ideas for movies and plays. Dennis had been to our home in Solana Beach several times with Jimmy, but we hadn't heard from Dennis in over a year.

Now Dennis's voice shook as he said, "Mr. Gauntt, my mom called from Chicago this afternoon. A friend of hers described an amazing story told to him by a guy named George from Connecticut, about their high school classmate Casey, whose son Jimmy was struck by an automobile and killed in 2008. And then Casey got a letter his dad wrote to him forty years before, sent by a lady in West Virginia and he got it on his son's birthday."

"Oh, my God!" I exclaimed.

Dennis plunged on. "Mom was crying and asked, 'Wasn't that your friend, Jimmy? The one who came to visit us?' And I said yes. Mr. Gauntt, what's going on? Who is George? What's this story about a letter?"

I was absolutely incredulous and my head was spinning. "Dennis, slow down!" I implored. "Who told your mother about the letter?"

"Some friend of hers. I don't know his name."

I told Dennis I had reconnected with my old friend Blystone only a week earlier. "I'll send you the story I wrote about the letter."

Something very strange and exciting was going on, but I was confused. Who told Dennis's mother about Jimmy and the letter from my dad? I fired off an e-mail to George and asked, "When you were in Chicago, who did you tell about the letter? I've got a story that will knock your socks off."

George called me back a couple of days later. He explained he had been having a glass of wine with our classmate Jerry at the Palmer House in Chicago when I had called. He was in the middle of telling Jerry about Jimmy and the letter. George swore Jerry was the only person he'd told the story to. "Casey, I read your story and was still crying when I got on the plane for Chicago. I haven't even told my wife."

As he told Jerry about Jimmy, Jerry's mouth dropped open and his eyes widened. "I know about this!" he said. It turns out Dennis's mother was a good friend of Jerry's and had told him about the tragedy shortly after it happened, and how devastated her son Dennis was over Jimmy's death.

The circle began and completed itself like this. I send *The Letter* to George, George meets with Jerry, Jerry then calls Dennis's mother and tells her about his meeting with George, that he and Casey had been classmates, that Casey is Jimmy's dad, Mrs. Kim calls her son Dennis, Dennis calls me, and I send him the story of *The Letter*. From San Diego to Connecticut to Chicago to Los Angeles, to San Diego and back to L.A. in eight days? That's some kind of ride.

I told George about my call from Dennis on Tuesday.

George was stunned, to say the least. "What are the odds of us all being connected through Jimmy? I'll tell you. Incalculable! There's something going on here that's much bigger than you and me, my friend."

THE FRATERNITY

BACK IN MY college days at USC, I was proud to be a member of my fraternity, Delta Tau Delta, aka The Delts. My brother was also a Delt at SC. My pledge nickname was "Big Grover." My brother never used that name for me. After Jimmy died, I found I had joined another fraternity: fathers who have lost children. Logically, I knew I wasn't the only parent to have lost a child, but it sure as hell felt like it. Then I discovered so many of those close to me—and some not so close—had suffered mightily, too.

In June 2001 Richard Page's only son, Alex, was a passenger in a car heading for the beach. Alex was eighteen years old, with his first year of college under his belt. His friend lost control driving down a steep road in Solana Beach, the car struck a pole and flipped. The driver survived.

Brittany's high school graduation in 1998 and Jimmy's in 2002 bracketed Alex's graduation in 2000. They all went to Torrey Pines High School. When they were kids, Brittany played on the same soccer team as Alex's sister, Jessica. Hilary and I had gone to dinner with Richard and his wife years before. Richard is also a lawyer in San Diego, and we ran into each other occasionally.

Of course we had heard about Alex's death but I never spoke to Richard about it, just as I had never commiserated with our dentist when his four-year-old son was killed while digging a backyard "cave" that collapsed on him. I'd been going to him for eight years, and they lived in the town next door, Del Mar. I found a new dentist. I had also hidden from the discomfort of bringing up with my physician of twenty-five years his teenage son's suicide. I couldn't face the elephant in the room. I was crippled by the same misconceptions and bad assumptions that most of our friends and colleagues held after Jimmy died: *I don't know what to say. It will be too painful if I bring it up. I can't go to that dark and frightening place. If I don't talk about it, they can get on with their lives. It's better for them if we don't bring it up.* Complete bullshit.

The elephant is always in the room, and it never goes away.

Richard called me unexpectedly the day after Jimmy died. His call could have been lost in the muddled memories of hundreds of other calls and people dropping by, but something he said struck a chord. "You are now a member of the shittiest fraternity there is, my friend, the fraternity nobody wants to join, and God forbid they ever have to. I feel so sorry for you right now. You have no idea how hard it's going to be. But I do, and that's why I'll be calling you every so often to check in and see how you are doing."

And he did.

Early on, he had asked me if I planned to bring legal action against the drivers who had struck Jimmy. I knew that his situation was different, but I said, "It was nobody's fault. They were unfortunately in the same place at the wrong time." A couple of years later I re-read an e-mail exchange I had with Richard about five Torrey Pines High School kids who had been in a traffic accident in October 2009 after a party. One of them, also named Alex, was killed.

Hilary and I were in Coalwood meeting up with Emily Sue at the time of the accident, so when I got back I sent Richard an e-mail, knowing it struck way too close to home for him and his wife, Sandy. He fired an e-mail right back. "Every time another needless death strikes our community, I go back down that rabbit hole."

Now I thought, *I haven't had any contact with Richard for over a year. I should give him a call.* Of course, I got busy and didn't get around to making that call.

An hour later, my phone rang. It was Richard on his cell. He was upbeat. "Guess where I was? I just spent an hour having coffee with Greg Post. Do you know who he is?"

"No, but I can never forget what happened." Four months earlier a horrific accident had taken the life of Greg's eighteen-year-old daughter, Amanda, as she and some other recent graduates of nearby Cathedral High were returning from a track clinic in Mammoth. Amanda was a high school track star and she would be entering Cal Poly San Luis Obispo in the fall on a full-ride track scholarship. The driver of the SUV she was in lost control, crossed the median, and collided head-on with a van. Four died and the others were critically injured. Amanda's boyfriend, Derek, survived the crash—barely—but was burned over eighty-five percent of his body. The accident occurred on August 9, 2010. Two years to the day after Jimmy's death.

When Hilary and I heard the news, we both bemoaned, "It's their day one." Day one of the beginning of the nightmare for the parents, families, and friends—the day their lives were changed forever.

Richard continued. "I don't know Greg, either. But I called him up and invited him for coffee. It's one of the things I do. It's very rough for him. Like it was for you."

"You won't believe this," I said, "but not an hour ago I thought about calling you!"

"Synchronicity," he said. "Carl Jung wrote a paper about it. Read it."

I was surprised by the number of fraternity brothers who lived nearby. Bill and Cathie Canepa live a block away from us. We met them a week after Jimmy died. They came by to offer condolences and to let us know they had lost their son, Sean, four months earlier to an accidental drug overdose. He was eighteen. We found out later Anthony Ortega played at Bill and Cathie's wedding. Gary and Kay Weiss live in nearby Rancho Santa Fe. They lost their son Michael, around the same time as Sean, also to an accidental drug overdose. Michael was a freshman at USC, and Jimmy played football at Torrey Pines with his older brother Justin. We were friends. I saw Gary at the U.S. Open at Torrey Pines Golf Club in June 2008. I veered away so I wouldn't have to talk to him. I'm not sure if he saw me. I didn't get far. Two months later we hugged and cried and talked about our sons at Jimmy's memorial service.

Hugh Sill and I are members of the same two fraternities. Hugh is from Bakersfield in the California central valley and we were both Delts at USC. In those early dark weeks after my father died, Hugh was very kind and drove me up to Springville to visit my sister and mother, who had moved in with her folks. Unfortunately Hugh found out the hard way about the cause of my dad's demise. I, of course, hadn't told him. When he asked my mom what happened, she fired back, "Grover shot himself." Hugh was crushed, and I felt bad. We picked pineapples together in Maui the following summer and stayed close for several years following graduation until we had a falling out over something that doesn't matter anymore.

In the early 1990s I had heard that one of Hugh's sons, aged four, had fallen in a swimming pool and suffered severe brain damage. George would live for another ten years. I did not reach out to Hugh after his son passed away. Two years after Jimmy died and I became a member of our other fraternity, Hugh reached out to me. Our friendship was instantly rekindled and he taught me about their special love for George, who depended upon them for everything, and the smiles he gave them in gratitude for their love. We talk about our sons and our grandchildren.

One of my other dual fraternity brothers was Bill Driscoll. Bill was a year behind me in the Delt House and he married Hilary's best friend and sorority sister, Ludie Callahan, the funniest woman I know. Bill and Ludie's son, Brian, was born with a bad heart and he received a heart transplant when he was twelve. Although donors were anonymous, the day they received the call that a heart had been found for Brian, Ludie saw an article in the Los Angeles Times about a thirteen year old girl that had been killed when she was thrown from a roller coaster at an amusement park in San Jose. The article said the family had donated her organs and Ludie figured Brian would be receiving that girl's heart. After the operation, Ludie told Brian the story and he expressed some concern about now having the heart of a girl. Ludie reassured him, "Oh honey, there's nothing for you to worry about. Now, just so you know, you will begin to menstruate in a few months."

Brian and Jimmy were the same age. Hilary and I regretted not being able to donate Jimmy's organs. The Medical Examiner's decision to do an autopsy precluded that opportunity. They found Jimmy had well over twice the legal limit of alcohol in his bloodstream at the time of the accident—nothing else. Brian put up a valiant fight and lived five more years until the heart of the friend he had not met could beat no more. He was seventeen. I was busy with work or something and couldn't make it to Brian's service.

Eight years later in May 2009, Bill suffered a massive, fatal heart attack. I went to his service at the Holy Family Catholic Church in South Pasadena. Several of my Delt brothers and Hilary's Delta Gamma sorority sisters were there, as they had been for Hilary and me at Jimmy's memorial service nine months earlier. One of the rituals of passing from Delt pledge to an active member is a ceremony called the "Ring of Fire." It's disgusting and slightly sick but it's tradition and was preceded by twelve hours of non-stop playing at eardrum-busting levels of Johnny Cash's song of the same name. Back in our days, any Delt from USC would, when they heard that song, cringe and be reminded of that burning pain like no other in the place where you sit down. I will say no more about that.

Which brings me back to the funniest woman I know. After Monsignor Clement Connolly delivered the benediction of a deeply moving and powerful service for Bill in one of the most grandiose cathedrals in the Los Angeles area, and as we tearful mourners began to stand and slowly file into the aisles, a band of ten mariachis whom no one had before seen stood up in the balcony and played "Ring of Fire" as loudly as possible. Our tears turned to cheers and every Delt brother joined in and sang that song at the top of our lungs. Thank you, Ludie. It was exactly how "Billy D" would have wanted to exit.

We recently did some remodeling work on our house, and our contractor told us a story of some family problems he was addressing. We thought it a bit odd that a guy we had just met would be sharing something so personal with us. We hadn't told him anything about ourselves or our son.

As Bill measured and took notes, he noticed the picture of Jimmy with his saxophone on the piano. "My son plays alto sax," he said. "He's majoring in music in Texas." Out of nowhere he followed up with this: "My brother-in-law was struck by a drunk driver while walking home from a party and was almost fully paralyzed. He was twenty-four when that happened. He's fifty-four now. His mother—my wife's mom—passed away last week. We had to put him in a facility because he needs someone to feed and dress him." He paused for a moment. "His mom devoted the rest of her life, and probably shortened it, to take care of her son, Jimmy."

I'm actually proud that Hilary and I didn't break down. That could have been us: Jimmy, broken but still alive. I thought of George Sill and Brian Driscoll. Were Richard Page, Greg Post, and I better off having our children leave so quickly, and not suffering as their bodies slowly gave out? Would we give anything for one more day with our son or daughter, one more hug, one more kiss? You bet we would—in a heartbeat. There is no "better" way to lose a child. There's no barometer of pain. Our suffering is no more or less than Hugh's, Ludie's, or any other parent who loses a child. We walk arm and arm together with our loss and we help each other. That's what fraternity brothers do.

On December 22, 2014, I came into the office and pulled up an e-mail from George Blystone that he had sent the night before. "If you have time call me tomorrow at the office. I need some advice."

I called George right away. When he picked up, his voice was tired and shaky, devoid of all humor. "Hey, pal. I joined your fraternity. Our daughter Remy died two weeks ago of a brain aneurism. I'm desperate for a sign from her, like you got from Jimmy. What do I do now?"

Thirty-four, same age as our Brittany. I broke down before I could answer his question.

JIMMY'S LEGACY

W

E ALWAYS KNEW that Jimmy was bright, committed, focused, and kind, but it was only after he left us that we realized just how much he meant to others. To be sure, we lost Jimmy when he died, but we also found him, the kind of man he had become, as person after person—people we knew, many we didn't—showed up and told us about the ways Jimmy had deeply touched their lives.

In the spring of 2005 Hilary and I went to a small theatre on USC's campus to attend the premier performance of Jimmy's first play, *The Leather Clad Chaperone*. Evan Nicholas was the play's director, and Jimmy and he cast the play with members of USC's theatre and music departments. They were beside themselves when this gorgeous blond from Texas tried out for the leading role of Ana, the anopheles mosquito, and completely bowled over when she accepted. They all went down to Frederick's of Hollywood to buy her skin-tight, skimpy, black leather dominatrix costume and whip. The house was packed with friends and family, as well as connoisseurs of great art. As we made our way to our seats, a man approached us and introduced himself as Professor David Roman of SC's English department. He quickly got to the point of telling us that Jimmy was one of the three best students he had ever had over his many years of teaching, including his tenure at Yale. When we tried to thank him, he said, "I'm not telling you this to be nice. Jimmy is an extraordinary writer. He can make a career with his talent." And with that he turned away and walked to his seat.

Although *Leather Clad* closed the following night to another standing room only crowd, the casting of Alyson Weaver as Ana turned out to be one of Jimmy's and Evan's best decisions. Evan and Alyson were married on December 31, 2013, in the First Congregational Church of Los Angeles— the same church my folks were married in sixty-seven years earlier.

Six months after Jimmy died, Professor Roman wrote to tell us that he and USC's English department were creating an annual award to be given to the most outstanding graduating seniors majoring in English. "Jimmy was an amazing young man who made a lasting impression upon everyone who met him. I want to pay tribute to his tremendous talent by establishing this award in his honor. I think the USC students will also be inspired by it. The award will be known as the James Gauntt Memorial Award, but everyone is already referring to it as 'The Jimmy.' I hope you approve," he wrote.

We did.

The first annual James T. Gauntt Memorial Award dinner was held on May 3, 2010, at Ristorante Zucca, a lovely Italian bistro in downtown Los Angeles. In attendance were the five inaugural winners of The Jimmy, seven English professors, including Professor Roman, Brittany, nine months pregnant, Ryan, Hilary, and I. It was truly a magical evening. Each recipient was introduced and his or her qualifications and achievements were presented by a professor. Although they all received monetary awards and certificates, the students made a point to emphasize they were most thankful and proud of having their professors stand up and sing their praises in such a warm and intimate environment. Each said, in one way or another, "I've never had a teacher do that before." Professor Roman spoke so beautifully and admirably about Jimmy the student, the writer, his friend. He couldn't stop crying. We wept, we remembered, we wanted to comfort him. It was a beautiful and deeply powerful moment of personal acknowledgment, recognition, and connection.

Before the close of the dinner I stood up and shared with the group something I had found a few days earlier. Other than Hilary, no one in the room had seen or heard of it before.

"I kept this in a file labeled 'Jimmy L.A. Star' with several of his other writings because I thought someday Jimmy will be famous and people will want to read these. I just figured it would be fifty years from now. I'd like to read it to you."

From: James Gauntt

Sent: Wednesday, September 29, 2004 11:27 p.m.

To: Hilary Gauntt; Gauntt, Casey

Subject: bragging rights

Attachment: American Lit paper

Hi, guys. Well, I guess I have to tell you guys because I have to tell someone, and I can tell you. I turned in my paper to the American Lit class yesterday, and I think it's the best paper I've ever written. So I'm walking through the halls today and I run into my professor, who proceeds to tell me (and I'm not exaggerating) that this paper was beautiful, that everything I've said in the class had been utterly brilliant, and that he is so thankful he taught this class this semester for the privilege of having met me. I swear to God, that's what he said. Then I started to be very humble, and he wouldn't listen to any of it, and just walked away. It's a great memory. I'm almost scared to show him my plays, now! Love you guys, Jimmy"

I continued. "An immensely powerful and unforgettable moment between an aspiring student-writer and a professor. Attached to the e-mail was the paper Jimmy wrote for American Literature 263 during his junior year at USC. His professor? David Roman. That moment six years ago was the crucible of The Jimmy Award—that moment when a professor intersects the life of his student at that perfect time with praise and encouragement that emboldens him to pursue his dreams and ambitions. We are here tonight because of that moment between Jimmy Gauntt and Professor Roman."

⁓ 🙶🙷 ⁓

Thanks to Brittany's brainstorm on our walk at the San Elijo Lagoon that first day after Jimmy's accident, Hilary and I were on our way to the annual awards program at Torrey Pines High School in June 2013. This was our fifth year. The first year, Ryan had presented the James Tedrow Gauntt Memorial Scholarships because for Hilary and me, the wounds were still too raw. We could not speak of him without falling apart. So our son-in-law stepped up to the plate, as he always has, and represented the family. The tradition continued for the next three years.

Evening rush hour was in full swing, and we fretted that we wouldn't arrive in time. Fortunately we got there with minutes to spare, to be greeted by a covey of parents and students eagerly waiting in front of the gym.

We had asked the four recipients of this year's Jimmy scholarships to meet us outside so we could introduce ourselves. We offered quick congratulations to Charlie Yang, Blair Cannon, Judy Kim, and Maya Pilevsky, then took a few pictures and hustled inside.

Bobbi Karlson, who runs the high school's foundation, breathed a huge sigh of relief when she saw us come through the door. She hurried to us and said, "You are the first presenters tonight! Where's Ryan?"

"He's got the flu," I said. "Sick as a dog."

"Then you'll just have to do it," Bobbi said, her tone and expression firm, as she hustled us toward the stage. We managed to get through the presentations—I choked up just once—and went back to our seats.

The master of ceremonies announced the next award. "The Amanda Post Memorial Scholarship, presented by Greg Post."

Hilary and I exchanged shocked glances. I fumbled with my program, sure we had heard it wrong. I looked up to see a man about my age make his way to the microphone and introduce himself. "Good evening. My name is Greg Post." Two fathers speaking two minutes apart, their children's deaths exactly two years apart. Time means nothing in the infinite scheme of meetings and separations.

As Greg spoke, I felt like I was buckling, falling in on myself. His openness and compassion stunned us, as did his composure as he described the amazing accomplishments of his daughter and the horror of the tragic accident that took her life and almost killed her boyfriend, Derek.

I sat there dumbfounded. Here was the guy Richard Page had had coffee with more than two years ago, the man I'd been thinking about contacting but had not. His daughter didn't even go to Torrey Pines High School. He was standing right in front of me—and I didn't go up to him.

I nudged Hilary. She already had her purse in her hands. Ignoring the looks we got from the audience, we made our way up the aisle. We had nowhere to go. We just couldn't be there anymore. I imagined Richard yelling at me. "Greg just got up in front of all of these people he doesn't know and who have no idea what he's been going through, and you run out the door? You are such a chicken shit!" And he was right.

We slunk home. Upstairs in the living room, we watched as the setting sun dropped toward the smooth-like-glass Pacific. The humidity, the low scattered clouds, refracted the light in a way we had not seen—or noticed—before. The last rays of the sun lit up a five foot by ten foot painting hanging in the dining room. Rod Knutson painted it in 2006, a fantastical family portrait. I had given him photos of us, Hilary's folks, my mom, and Ryan.

Rod had painted all of us as restaurant patrons and owners sitting and standing at outdoor tables in a small town in Provence as a woman leads a flock of sheep on the narrow cobbled street in front of the restaurant. The shepherdess and the waiter on the far right are not family members. Rod just painted them in, or so he says. Each of us is easily recognizable in the painting, everyone except a twenty-two-year-old Jimmy. When we asked Rod about it he said, "Jimmy was changing so quickly I just couldn't capture him." He stands to the right, under an umbrella, hands on his aproned hips, ready to wait on his customers who have yet to arrive. He is the only one in the painting standing in the light, and the only sheep that has raised its head is looking right at Jimmy.

The orange sun hit the painting like a spotlight, and Jimmy and the umbrella were on fire. They shimmered, demanding our attention. In seven years I had never seen it—him—lit up so. Stunned, I grabbed my iPhone and hastily snapped a few inadequate mementos. The light faded, and the tears came.

Of course Jimmy would be with us in spirit this night. The portal had been thrown open once again, though it took a couple of days for it to sink in because we were still reeling from the mountain of emotions pressing upon us.

Bill Harris, who started the Allen Matkins law firm's San Diego office with me back in 1987, e-mailed me the next day. As a wee lad, Jimmy got to know Bill and, like the rest of us, thought of him as one of the funniest guys there is, and moreover as one of those special people, one of the good guys.

We had gone our own ways several years ago and, although we run into each other on the rare occasion, I was surprised to get an e-mail from him. What he had to say knocked me off my feet. He, his wife, and daughter were at the awards ceremony the night before. He praised my speech, which I barely remembered, and the wonderful way we kept Jimmy's spirit alive through the scholarship program.

Then he hit me with an oh-by-the-way postscript. "After Jimmy's memorial service I was home alone for a couple of days… I needed to do something beautiful in honor of Jimmy… on the side of our house I created a little landscaped garden in his honor… I see it every day… and I think of Jimmy and your family." He had planted an angel's trumpet tree and lots of white roses, and added a little bird bath. "As long as we are in our house, I will make sure it lives on and thrives just as Jimmy and all his accomplishments (and great memories) will live on forever."

Through my tears, I realized what I had to do: No more spiritual head thumps required. I got Greg Post's e-mail from Bobbi and sent off this message.

"Dear Greg—I wanted to commend you for standing up before everyone last night and honoring and remembering your daughter, Amanda, and her friends in such a moving and beautiful way. You displayed such courage and composure, and I know only too well how difficult that can be. Your daughter's tragic death resonated very deeply with our family, and I think about you often, and always on one day in particular. Our son Jimmy also passed on August 9, in 2008. I've been meaning to reach out to you for a long time... last night I would have introduced myself, but we had to leave early for another engagement." My cowardice still had a grip on me, but it was loosening. "Do you want to have coffee one of these days? We have some things we can talk about, I'm sure."

Hilary and I had breakfast with Greg and Missy Post a few weeks later. We spent two hours honoring our two kids who somehow had touched and changed the lives of thousands of people in their very short time here. Before we hugged and said goodbye, Greg said, "I guess we're in the same fraternity, aren't we?"

A week after the awards at the high school, we received an e-mail from Maya Pilevsky, one of The Jimmy Scholarship recipients. She wrote of how much it meant to have her accomplishments as an artist publicly rewarded, since most people's reaction was to tell her to do something better with her life, get a stable job and a steady income. She spoke of a compatriot, Marinee, who had a quote from Jimmy's poem, "Suffering is the Only Honest Work," tattooed on her forearm: *Doubt is a bad idea*. She went on, "Those words have become a mantra for me and other Torrey Pines Players [the school drama club]... It simply would be an insult to my intellect to know what I love to do and run from it out of fear of failure."

This was precisely how Jimmy explained his calling to be an artist to his family and friends. Maya had just beautifully and eloquently validated the very reason why The Jimmy Scholarship Award was originally envisioned by Brittany.

But the *Doubt Is A Bad Idea* tattoo was completely and utterly out of the blue.

Marinee has been a teacher at Torrey Pines for several years. She's an institution at the school and runs the theatre department. We may have met her once or twice. Jimmy didn't get involved in theatre until his senior year, but Marinee worked with him on the bit parts he had in two plays that year. In spite of his success as an athlete, he was becoming an artist.

He was changing. He had not fully discovered this, not like Maya, but the caterpillar was spinning his cocoon.

How did Marinee get Jimmy's poem? Why had we not heard anything about the tattoo? Marinee wasn't the only one with a "Jimmy" tattoo. Ali Eastman, a close friend of Jimmy's since high school, got a tattoo on her wrist of the word "Love" in Jimmy's handwriting from a note he had sent to her. Steven Tran, another good pal from high school, tattooed "Bravo, Jimmy" on his forearm. Those were the words I shouted as I rose to my feet at the close of Jimmy's memorial service. One thousand others rose with me and gave Jimmy his duly deserved standing ovation at the Mandeville Auditorium. We were humbled.

Even Jimmy's last few hours inspired a movie. Jimmy met Joe Carnahan through Evan Nicholas, who was working as Joe's assistant. Evan and Jimmy ghostwrote an action/adventure screenplay for Joe. It's not yet a movie, but who knows? Maybe one day.

After Jimmy passed away, Joe Carnahan co-wrote and directed the movie, *The Grey*. The film's leading man, Liam Neeson, and his crew of oil field roughnecks are flying home for some R&R when their plane crashes in the hinterlands of northern Alaska. Within hours they are confronted with a pack of starving wolves. Over the next several days, as each man is torn apart by the predator he has feared since childhood, Liam collects his wallet.

At the Los Angeles premiere Carnahan talked about how the script came to be. "A guy I work with, a very dear friend of mine, we had a mutual friend and a very young guy. He was twenty-four at the time and he passed away rather suddenly and rather dramatically. He just had too much to drink one night and walked out of a house, and instead of going left, he went right, and that was the end of it. He wound up being killed by a passing car.

"My friend remembers going to his home, going to his apartment after that and seeing there was still a Led Zeppelin LP on his turntable and still the signs of life and still these little notes he had written to himself.

And I always thought, it's just so heartbreaking to me, you know, that's the measure of the end."

With that inspiration, in the final scene Neeson spreads all of the wallets he has collected on the ground and looks through their contents as he awaits the wolf pack to close in and finish off the lone survivor. The photos from the wallets that play at the end of the film are real photographs of the actors and their families.

Besides packing two lifetimes of learning and creating into a couple of decades, Jimmy inspired so many others to follow their dreams and do their best. Through The Jimmy Awards at USC and The Jimmy Gauntt Memorial Scholarships at Torrey Pines High School, he'll continue to do so forever.

—◦◦◦—

Richard Page, Greg Post, and I held the first gathering of our fraternity in August 2013 at the Lodge at Torrey Pines, with spectacular views of the North and South golf courses and Pacific Ocean. We talked a lot about our kids: how much we miss them, how we deal with our loss, that we never want to forget, and what we do to remember them.

Richard rolled up his sleeve and showed us a tattoo on his forearm: the outline of a wave and the initials AP. "Alex liked to sign letters and notes with a wave and his initials. This is from the note he left us the day he was killed. This is his handwriting." Richard's voice broke.

Greg, not missing a beat, rolled up his sleeve to show us the tattoo on his forearm. A yellow apple rested against a gothic capital letter A. The words *Amanda Post* were next to it. "This is how Amanda signed her letters and this is her handwriting." Richard quickly observed, "Our kids have the same initials—AP." My brothers looked to me as if to say, "Your turn." I stood up in the middle of the posh club bar, took off my shirt, and turned around. On my back was my still-fresh tattoo: *Suffering Is The Only Honest Work—Jimmy.* Jimmy typed the body of the poem but handwrote the title and his signature. Three dads—three tattoos—all in the handwriting of their children. We will never forget. And why would we ever want to?

AGENTS OF ANGELS

THERE'S A GREAT country song by the group Alabama called "Angels Among Us," which tells of strangers, mysterious and otherwise, who change lives just by being kind. Of course, angels aren't limited to strangers; one of my favorite angels is Emily Sue Buckberry. She would never apply that appellation to herself. She's too humble and down to earth to consider herself to be a messenger from heaven. When I mentioned her halo, she laughed. "I'm *not* an angel. But agent of an angel, that's okay. I can go with that."

When she chose to pick up my dad's letter from beside the wastebasket outside my room at the Clubhouse in Coalwood all those years ago, she never thought, *Gee, I better keep this because Casey's dad is going to die in a couple of years and then his son is going to be killed forty years from now and I'll return it to him then when he'll really appreciate it.* That's not to say someone or something wasn't thinking this at that moment, but she clearly wasn't conscious of it.

John Davies and Ron Roberts were two of our early angels, performing herculean tasks to get us into the Medical Examiner's office to see our son. Chaplain Joe Davis was another when he took Hilary's and my hands and challenged us to beat the odds and stay together.

In a broader sense, there are angels or agents of angels among us every moment of every day. Perhaps each one of us is, or has the opportunity to be, an agent. Opportunities constantly present themselves for each of us to do something good, purposeful, and perhaps life changing for us or someone else. Sometimes they're right in front of you. What will you do with them?

A stranger, maybe a homeless person, stumbles and collapses on a crowded sidewalk. Do you stop and help or do you walk by, rationalizing that *Somebody else will stop*. What if there is no one else around? Do you walk on? You may think, *He's a stranger. I don't want to get involved. I've got an urgent appointment. I'll be late. I'm afraid.*

So often we dismiss the interconnectedness of humanity, using our sensible minds to avoid involvement. But consider this scenario. Maybe that old bum isn't a stranger. Maybe he was a very close friend of your brother who passed away three years ago in a car accident. Maybe that bum was your brother's age. Maybe he recently lost his job and was suffering from depression that had deepened because of your brother's death. Maybe he had something to tell you, had he known how to get hold of you, about your brother, something wonderful that now you will never know.

Why did Emily Sue decide to send the letter when she did? Why not ten years earlier or five years later? Why, precisely, at that particular moment? Think of the decision tree in front of her: "He'll think this is so weird that I kept it all these years. He'll think I'm weird" or "He'll be mad. 'Who gave you the right to pick up and keep the letter for all these years?'" or "He won't remember me. I'll mail it to him anonymously."

That's probably what I would have done, if I had decided to do anything at all. But she called. And she walked up to that man, whom she did not yet know was crumpled on the street, and said, "I have something you left behind in Coalwood and I need to return it to you." With Emily, it was making that leap and connection without consciously knowing why or for what purpose other than this was the right thing to do, something she had meant (or was meant) to do for a long, long time.

A few years ago I was driving home from work. As I approached the freeway exit to our house, a song by Dawes, "A Little Bit of Everything," was playing on the radio and Taylor Goldsmith was singing the line in that song about an old homeless man standing in a food serving line at a shelter. "Making up for when his bright future left him, Making up for the fact his only son is gone." Thanks to Brittany and Jimmy's friend, Ryan Richter, a few months earlier we had the Dawes bandmates to our house for dinner, and then headed over to the Belly Up nightclub a few blocks away and watched them play. Taylor dedicated that song in memory of Jimmy Gauntt.

I started to cry and by the time I hit the stoplight at the end of the exit I was sobbing my guts out. Standing on the corner was a disheveled homeless man, his age hard to gauge because of the wear and tear of the streets and a life lived hard. Tears running down my face, I powered down my window and beckoned him over. As I handed him a twenty, he looked straight into my eyes and with a voice as clear and sober as the day is long said to me, "You're going to be all right, man." And I was awash in goose bumps for the rest of the drive home.

We all have these moments and opportunities at our fingertips. The call we've been thinking about making to that old friend. The conversation we've thought about starting with that person we don't yet know. Our preconceptions, based on our skewed mental constructs and filters, keep us from connecting with those around us. We see the person who works out next to us at the gym, to whom we've never spoken, and think, *He never makes eye contact. He must be emotionally disturbed, or, She never smiles. She's an unhappy person.* Then we share our opinions with others, and thus compound the disparagement.

We think nothing of e-mailing and texting and chattering on about nothing as we seek to be recognized by those around us. We don't hesitate to call to congratulate someone on his achievement or victory (especially when we think it may be of benefit to us), or bask in the glow of her accomplishment. Yet we hesitate to compliment a loved one. We vacillate over offering encouragement or advice to a friend or acquaintance. We falter over the small task of just being there when someone needs us. Then, when it's too late, a twinge or even a tsunami of guilt and regret sweeps over us. Why didn't we call her when she lost her job, or her brother, or simply her way?

What is it that makes an Emily Sue Buckberry pick up the phone and call? I think she learned valuable lessons from her friend Homer "Sonny" Hickam. His books and memoirs told a truth about Coalwood, his family, and dear friends. He recognized and included them in his story, which is compelling and moving because of its simplicity and its honesty. Sonny went to the edge and wasn't afraid to tell his story, talk about his dad, and share his strengths as well as his frailties and misgivings. He showed Emily that reaching out and through is good, even if you can't predict the consequences. I think Emily is also a very strong woman, with a strong mind, confidence, a deep well of compassion, and a sense of destiny and purpose of doing something that may be acknowledged as important and memorable. She is one with and true to herself, going with her instincts. Without this combination of strong people like Sonny and Emily, and their friendship that started many years before I arrived in town, I probably never would have received the letter, or connected with my dad and son, and never had the chance to share it.

I probably never would have dealt with the truth about my father's death. I never would have come to understand that life flows on, either on this plane or the next, and that we never really lose those we love. We find them and they find us.

Another real angel delivered some terrifically exciting news in 2009. During the summer of 2009, Ryan and Brittany started trying to conceive a child. During the early-morning hours of September 2, she had a dream that would change her life. Brittany had only had a couple dreams of Jimmy in the year since he had died. But I think this story is best told in her words.

"In this particular dream, my ten-year-old brother appeared to deliver a very important message. Jimmy was wearing his Little League uniform and had a beautiful and bright white light behind him. He had a big smile on his face and his crystal blue eyes were piercing. Eagerly, Jimmy said, 'Britt, you're pregnant. And you're going to have a boy!'

"I sat straight up in bed and looked at the clock, which read seven a.m. I needed to use the bathroom. Still reeling from the vividness of the dream and the news my brother had so enthusiastically delivered, I decided to take a pregnancy test. My heart raced as I took the test, yet time crawled as I paced around my bedroom, waiting for the stick to dry. In a few moments, I hurried back to look at the stick. Two thin blue lines! I yelped with joy and excitement and hurried into the living room to share the joyous news with Ryan. He was thrilled! And amazed by Jimmy's appearance in my dream. However, we would have to wait a few months to confirm the sex of our child.

"Four months into our pregnancy, I lay still as an ultrasound technician ran the lubricated wand over my abdomen. Ryan stood beside me, holding my hand, and my mom and dad peered at the screen where my child kicked and squirmed

"As the baby twisted and turned, the tech said, 'Are you ready to find out what you're having?'

"'Yes!'

"She paused for a second, then announced, 'It's a boy!'

"Tears came, and I recalled Jimmy's sweet face and words in my dream. Of course, Jimmy, my only sibling, would want to share this experience with me, one of the most momentous and magical of my life. He wouldn't miss it for the world."

Brittany and Ryan welcomed a healthy baby boy on May 14, 2010, and Wyatt James Kirby began a new chapter of this life and that of our family.

AFTERWORD

FOR THE LAST seven years I have felt Jimmy at my side moving the pen in my hand. So much of this book is his work and handiwork. His letters, plays, and poems including, in my opinion, his most powerful piece, *Suffering is the Only Honest Work*, to be sure, but it is much more than that. It's the work he has done after he left us that has blown the doors off our hearts and minds: his Moment In Paris with his mother and Aunt Laura, Jimmy coming into Brittany's dream foretelling her pregnancy with a boy, or just hanging out with us on the couch—his spot—in our house. I deeply felt something more powerful and otherworldly was involved. Hilary, Brittany, and I knew Jimmy and my father, somehow, were pulling the strings, and yet we were grateful to so many others with whom we shared our journey who assured us we had not completely lost our minds, including two Catholic priests.

Monsignor Clement Connolly of the Holy Family Church in South Pasadena, who presided over Bill Driscoll's memorial service, sent me a letter after he read the stories "The Letter," "Into The Light," and "The Rabbit Hole." He observed, "There is a world beyond our knowing—in rare and sacred moments it is revealed to us. There God dwells. From that place of mystery Jimmy is ever present to us. It takes pensive moments, a convergence of unexpected miracles and then the eyes of faith to see and feel and experience the Gospel according to Jimmy. Thank you for the blessing of your sharing. It is truly inspiring."

The late Father Patrick O'Malley, who back in 1967 toured Ernie Smersky and me through the Chicago South Side as it was locked in the grips of race riots, offered his perspective. "When you are a beginner in the spiritual quest, things happen. And it is only on later reflection that you say, 'That really was a God-moment.' As you go along, however, you begin to recognize the God-moments ever more readily. Pretty soon, you are almost anticipating them—and they occur in greater numbers than you ever realized. Is that what is happening to you and your friends in The Fraternity? Has the tragedy of lost loved ones moved you to a different plane, with different understandings? Is Jimmy at work? These are not just rhetorical questions, Casey. Something is happening in your lives that, it seems from your writings, you need to continue to look at."

One of the most poignant scenes in the movie *Interstellar* is when Cooper (Matthew McConaughey) ejects from his spaceship and finds himself in a Tesseract, a fifth-dimensional place deep within a black hole where the laws of time and space don't apply. Cooper is floating on the "other" side of a bookshelf in his house back on Earth, and as he looks through gaps between the books he sees his daughter, Murph, as a young girl and a mature woman. He pushes books off the shelf and is somehow able to communicate with and get a message to Murph that will save the human race. The power of love plays a key role in all of this.

That scene comes as close as anything I've seen or heard to what may be happening to us. From the other side Jimmy, as well as my father, are making things happen on this side to communicate and connect with us. My father puts a letter in the hands of Emily Sue Buckberry in 1968 so she can get it to his son forty years later on the day it will mean the most to him. Jimmy calls his best friend John Dale on Christmas. Jimmy helps us find just the right photos of him on his spot on the couch to send to Steve Date for the film *The Letter*. On his twenty-fifth birthday, Jimmy draws attention to the book *Siddhartha* sitting on the shelf in Ryan and Brittany's house that contains the card he gave to Brittany on *her* twenty-fifth birthday.

Jimmy has pushed the "books"—stories he has scripted—off the shelves and into our laps with a message delivered to me loud and clear:

"Here you go, Dad. Write about this." Jimmy Gauntt justly deserves the bulk of the writing credit for this book, and in this case I think people will understand why I must include the name of my ghostwriter.

Bravo, Jimmy!

APPENDIX

HOW TO WRITE A BEAUTIFUL CONDOLENCE CARD TO SOMEONE WHO HAS LOST A CHILD

I WISH I didn't have so much experience on this subject. Our family received hundreds—maybe a thousand—cards and letters after Jimmy died. Since then I have lost my mother, my best friend, and a twenty-three-year-old niece. My father-in-law died on my sixty-first birthday and other family members and good friends have lost spouses, siblings, and parents. There has not been, nor will there ever be, a shortage of occasions to receive and express condolences, and probably nothing harder to write than a card or letter to someone who has lost a child.

Why is this so hard? The death of a child or young adult is just plain wrong. It's beyond the natural order of things. It's not supposed to happen, but it does. It's frightening, disorienting, and deeply unsettling for everyone caught in its wake. Many of the cards we received used the words "unthinkable" and "unimaginable." It's all of that and more. The pain and suffering of our family, our friends, and Jimmy's friends was palpable, like a writhing animal trapped in a deep shaft, denied all light, all air sucked out.

The screams and wails of those whom I called soon after the sheriff and medical examiner left will forever ring in my ears. The mask of shock and pain that instantly takes over the face of someone I've told for the first time that I lost my son, months and even years later, is never forgotten.

What can you possibly say or write to someone who has lost a child when you are dragged into your own nightmare just by thinking, *What if I lost one of my children or siblings?*

I completely get how hard it is to write something. As confessed in The Fraternity chapter, there were too many times I could not muster the courage to console fathers that I knew who had lost their sons. It took the death of my own son to realize my mistakes. I'll share some of what I wish I never learned and begin with some things to avoid.

- **Don't send an e-mail or post on a Facebook wall:** It reeks of being too easy and impersonal. Find a pen and write something. The handwritten word is very powerful; your energy and emotion are transferred to the paper through the pen. Although I vowed at the time to never re-read the cards and letters we got when Jimmy died, it is nice to have something that can be held and revisited.
- **Don't default to clichés:** "Words are inadequate… " or "Words cannot express… " Words are all you have when you write a card. "I cannot imagine what you are going through"; "I can only imagine the pain." If you haven't lost a child you can't—and shouldn't—try to put yourself in their shoes. Avoid stating the obvious.
- **Don't attempt to compare, rationalize, or project.** Don't try to make them feel better—you won't—and in those very early stages after their loss, you can't.
  - "Time heals all wounds." Time can never heal or erase the agony of losing a child. Those affected must come to terms with their loss in their own way without relying on time to take care of the process.
  - "I know he is in a better place." First of all, are you absolutely

positive about that? The obvious implication is that the recipients are in a worse place. In fact, they are in hell. It is not helpful to remind them of that.

- ° "God had a plan for her and needed to bring her home." Be careful of injecting your personal belief system unless you know for certain the recipient is on the same page. It's another one of those "Do you really have that level of firsthand knowledge?" sorts of things.

- ° Avoid bringing up in a card any loss you have suffered. You are writing a sympathy card, not an empathy card. The opening line of this card really jumped off the page for us: "I know the pain and suffering you are going through. Last month I had to put down my dog, Bippy, after 18 years." *What?* I know she didn't mean the loss of a dog and a child are the same, and I appreciate how people become deeply attached to and love their pets, and they too suffer when they lose them. But it's not the same. If you too have lost a child, there are other ways you can be of great assistance.

- **Don't be too hasty.** Your first instinct is to rush to the store, buy that card, scratch a few words inside, and get it in the mail the next day. We got an avalanche of envelopes within the first few days. The mail carriers certainly must know something bad has happened when they have to bring a box of mail to a doorstep because it won't fit in the mailbox. We wanted to read them—we were compelled to read each one of them—and yet I'm sure some very lovely messages simply were lost in the crowd of sorrow. Some of the ones we received later, like the one from Chris Cox, really stood out and meant a great deal to us.

It is also prudent to take your time with what you write and avoid the malapropisms that unfortunately occur, particularly in the midst of an emotional hurricane. One of our young family members closed his note of condolence regarding Jimmy's untimely death with "It couldn't have happened to a nicer guy." We knew what he meant to say. We actually got a good laugh from it, especially at a time we thought laughter had been forever taken away.

- **To you men:** We are generally horrible at expressing our feelings, showing our emotions, admitting our armor might have a chink. Don't always have your wife or significant other write the card, and no, a signature by itself doesn't cut it. We received precious few cards from the male species, and I can't tell you how much it meant to me when we did.

You are now probably saying, "With all these don'ts, it's safer to just get one of those Hallmark cards with the pre-printed message and sign it." Don't do that.

This is your opportunity to rise above the chaos, to express your love and friendship when they really need you to do that, to make it personal. This is your time to write something beautiful. Trust me. You can do it. As a man I have always appreciated examples. It just so happens, from the hundreds I received, I am able to share some touching and powerful illustrations with you.

So how do you write a condolence card that will stand out and be remembered? Let's start with the card my college fraternity brother Chris Cox wrote to us from Washington, DC, and examine the words and the structure.

Dear Casey and Hilary,

The news of Jimmy's loss is heartbreaking. Please know that Rebecca and I are thinking of you, and that there is boundless love and prayer being offered for your family from this side of the continent, too.

Your quarter century with Jimmy is an incredible gift—I know you realize that, and will always be grateful for the way he served such a high purpose in life, including helping you both to grow and learn and to expand and absorb your capacity to love.

You have so much to be proud of in Jimmy's life. And you have made me and all who know you proud, too, because we can see so much

of you both in Jimmy's many wonderful achievements, and in his
character, and sense of humor. In this time of sorrow, mixed with
gratitude for the sheer joy of Jimmy's life, please know we are with you.

—*Chris and Rebecca*

What made Chris's card special for us? I think it can be boiled down to these six things:

1. **Open strong with something from the heart:** Chris hand-wrote his letter to us on his personal stationery. There was no pre-printed message. He immediately started with an expression of his personal feelings about Jimmy's death. "The news of Jimmy's loss is heartbreaking... Rebecca and I are thinking of you and there is boundless love and prayer being offered for your family from this side of the continent." Here are some openings from other cards we received: "Our hearts ache for you." "We are devastated by Jimmy's death."

2. **Compliment the one who is gone:** Share a connection or memory you have with the child. "I know you... will always be grateful for the way he served such a high purpose in life... Jimmy's wonderful achievements and his character and sense of humor." Chris never met Jimmy and he likely based his observations on things he read or heard from others. Nevertheless, we appreciated his praise of our son. When we lost our son, I thought everything he was or did left with him. By sharing a compliment or a memory you are helping the bereaved stay connected with their child.

3. **Share a favorite memory of the child:** Write about an accomplishment, something funny he or she did. Share the connection you have with this person. "Jimmy was a student of mine in second grade and he always had his hand up first whenever I'd ask a question of the class—and he was almost always right!" "Jimmy and I played freshman football together at Torrey Pines High School. We were the smallest guys on the team, but nobody worked harder

or tried harder than Jimmy. He was fearless." If you don't know the child, try and find something online about him—an obituary is a very good source of information—and write about something you found interesting or that stands out. "I read that Jimmy was an accomplished jazz saxophone player. I've played the clarinet all my life and Charlie Parker is one of my all-time favorites."

4. **Compliment the parents or siblings:** "You have made me and all who know you proud, too, because we can see so much of you both in Jimmy's many wonderful achievements." The parents need support and praise in addition to your sympathy. This was from a letter one of my law partners wrote to me. "Casey, you are the most talented lawyer I know and it is no surprise that Jimmy excelled with his writing and acting. The apple didn't fall far from the tree."

   I know he didn't mean that—he's always thought he is a better lawyer—but it was still nice that he said it. If you know the parents well, express your love and friendship for them. Share a moment or a memory. Connect to them. You need to appreciate, even though you can't really understand, how lost and disconnected the parents and the siblings are. The world as they knew it has changed instantly and drastically. They are ships without sails tossed in a tumultuous sea. They have lost more than a child: They have lost their bearings, their direction. They no longer recognize the road before them. They are desperate for a hand—and a handhold. Reach out and grab them! "We've been friends for over 40 years. You were my best man and I stood up next to you at your wedding. We've laughed and cried together many times. The well of our friendship is deep and it will never run dry." If you are a good friend or family member, you will do more than write a letter. You will call them, go see them, walk with them, and pray with them—and you will do this over and over.

5. **Say something uplifting:** Chris wrote, "Your quarter century with Jimmy is an incredible gift. You will always be grateful for... [him] helping you both to grow and learn and expand and absorb your capacity to love... In this time of sorrow, mixed with gratitude

for the sheer joy of Jimmy's life, please know we are with you." The parents and siblings are drowning in sorrow and they need to be reminded there is more out there than darkness, even if they may not believe it when they read it. The sheer joy of Jimmy's life! Jimmy's life and ours with him was full of joy. It was brilliant of Chris to remind us of that. Note that Chris didn't speculate on where Jimmy might be or where we were at this moment. He made us focus on our moments with Jimmy, the things we knew.

6. **Take your time:** Chris obviously spent time thinking about what he wanted to say to us. He concisely conveyed many thoughts and feelings, and the labor of his writing was endearing and so impactful.

We received this card from our very good friends Diane and Greg Brown—Diane wrote the card. I think what really stood out for us was what a powerful and thoughtful writer Diane is. We didn't know she possessed this talent and were so taken with her eloquence and beautiful phrasing. We now see and think of her differently and with deeper regard and respect.

Dear Casey, Hilary, Brittany and Ryan,

There are never enough words to express our sorrow and the pain we share with you. We've been close friends for over 30 years and we will be here to support, comfort and love you now and forever. The memorial to Jimmy's life was filled with so much emotion. His very close friends who delivered remembrances gave us a glimpse into Jimmy's wonderful character, spirit and accomplishments. He brought such joy to everyone.

Greg and I loved speaking at length to Jimmy at Brittany and Ryan's wedding and now are so grateful to have spent those moments with him. Jimmy's words as illustrated in his plays and letters were astonishingly beautiful. He was an extraordinary son, brother and friend to all. We love you.

—Greg and Diane

Diane's card included the same six main ingredients of the card from Chris. She spoke from the heart—"the sorrow and the pain we share with you"—and when she wrote, "We love you," we knew she meant it. They complimented and shared a memory with Jimmy: the connection they made with Jimmy at the wedding, his wonderful character, and his beautiful writings. She spoke of their connection with us. "We've been friends for over 30 years and we will... love you forever," and included something uplifting: "He brought such joy to everyone." She clearly took her time and wrote the card a few days after the memorial service for Jimmy. Okay, she did open with the phrase "There are never enough words to express... " Still I give this card an A.

I also like that Diane addressed her letter to Jimmy's sister, Brittany, and his brother-in-law of less than a year, Ryan Kirby. Their pain and suffering was no less than ours. If you know the siblings in addition to the parents, think about writing a separate card or letter to them.

This card was from an old client of mine. Ron Hahn and his son, Ernie, were at Jimmy's memorial service. I clearly remember hugging them both. Jimmy and Ernie met a couple of times and Jimmy looked up to Ernie, fifteen years his senior. Ron wrote his card in a very painstaking, deliberate hand—also on personal stationery—and it was obvious he spent some time with it. And it was written by a guy!

Dear Casey and Hilary,

The three days since the memorial service have been sobering and uplifting for me. I never met or knew Jimmy, but after the service I felt I had known him forever. If a man is to be judged by his friends and family, Jimmy is to be judged at the highest level.

What a remarkable and talented son you raised. I can understand how emotional and painful that 1 ½ hours was for you both. You, however, honored him exceptionally. Regardless of his religious preferences, Jimmy was obviously outwardly and inwardly spiritual.

The shadow cast by his parents certainly allowed him to shine brightly

*in his world. Good for you both to have raised Jimmy to be his own
man and yet so remarkably like his parents.*

*Although this is certainly a life-changing experience for you both, I
know you will continue to be the exceptionally fine people that you are.*

We both hurt greatly for your loss. Love and Peace to you both.

—Ron and Linda

Ron spoke from the heart; he complimented Jimmy and us as parents. He wrote of the connection, the bond, between us and our son, and he included something uplifting: "Jimmy was obviously... spiritual" and "I know you will continue to be the exceptionally fine people that you are." Seeing Ron and Ernie at the service spoke volumes, and yet I never expected to receive a card like his. I'd known Ron for years, primarily in the business world. He was smart, sophisticated, and successful. I did not know the depth of Ron. He surprised me and wrote something beautiful.

To recap, you too can write a powerful condolence card to someone who has lost a child if you follow these six suggestions:
1. Open strong and say something from your heart.
2. Compliment the one who is gone.
3. Share a favorite memory or connection with the child.
4. Compliment the parents (or the siblings).
5. Say something uplifting.
6. Take your time.

Write something beautiful.

BOOKS THAT HELPED US

My Stroke of Insight Jill Bolte Taylor, Ph.D.
On Life After Death Elisabeth Kubler-Ross
On Grief and Grieving Elisabeth Kubler-Ross
Man's Search for Meaning Viktor E. Frankl
The Grief Recovery Handbook John W. James and Russell Friedman
Many Lives, Many Masters Brian L. Weiss, M.D.
Living When a Loved One Has Died Earl A. Grollman
Grieving Mindfully Sameet M. Kumar, Ph.D.
Walking in the Garden of Souls George Anderson and Andrew Barone
Spirited Rebecca Rosen
A Year of Magical Thinking Joan Didion
The Power of Now Eckhart Tolle
Co-Creating at Its Best (3 CD Set Lecture) Dr. Wayne W. Dwyer and Esther Hicks

Also: The guided imagery CDs from Health Journeys, which provide healing and relaxation through listening to Belleruth Naparstek's directed meditations. Affirmations are included at the end. These programs have been tested and found effective in numerous studies at major medical centers. We particularly benefited from the Healing Trauma (PTSD) CD.

FOR HENRI

By *James Gaunt*

WHEN I FIRST saw Henri, his withered body, a shell of its old self, had to be led carefully through the door by my father. Henri, an alto man, had been born in Paris, but the siren song of Dizzy and Duke lured him to the States. From then on his black leather case was his only companion, and his home was wherever his music, jazz music, was playing. Finally, the music had taken him to me.

At the beginning of our first lesson, Henri could barely play a chord. His tone was flat and sorrowful, the loneliness of his soul crying out through his song. His wilting, weathered face watched me play without care or compassion, all one could expect from someone with a broken heart. Jazz music had brought him to the ecstasy of original creation, but the jazz lifestyle had brought him near to death. He was lost in a world that had forgotten him, and I was one of his last stops on a journey no one was left to remember. My hands shook, reminding me of Henri's distress, and my pulse quickened, a hopeless attempt to speed up the slowing flow of life within him. Alone, I could do nothing to bring this man back to life, but the rescuing flight of a bird would do just the trick. The music of Charlie Parker, or "Bird," is an escape for the listener, for one gets lost in his twisting solos and driving tone. Henri and I certainly needed to flee the dark cavern of joyless music we were stuck in, and Parker was the only one who could help. At the end of the lesson, while trudging through exercises in the key of D, I started to play the classic Parker tune, "Now's The Time (no. 2)."

The short, staccato notes of the opening melody shocked the old jazzman, an alarm clock shrill to his creative hibernation. Waking from his sleep, Henri perked up, and from him came a rich tone of sound. He quickly joined me as we pounced on the melody. At the last of the first chorus, he authoritatively piled two G sharps right on top of each other, screaming through his music, "I'M BACK, BABY!"

The Bird spun us round and round through the melody, winding us tight, and then he let us go, releasing us full-bore into the solo as we held close to each other. Flying through the chords and attacking convention, our hearts soared to the heavens while our notes burned with fire. Henri was revitalized and refreshed, his spirit awakened by the controlled chaos of improvisation.

I realized then that I could never again let Henri leave my side. We had formed a musical bond that I could not bear to break. I kindly offered Henri a place in my home, and in my heart, for as long as he wished to stay. The twinkle in his ivory eyes gave me the answer I desired. I took a small sax-repair screwdriver out of Henri's case and looked down upon his glimmering face. Just underneath his embossment, "Henri Selmer Mark VII," and just above the phrase MADE IN FRANCE, I etched my initials, "JG," onto Henri. The old jazzman had finally found a home.

TO COUNT YOU A GREAT PROVIDER

By James T. Gauntt

[THIS WAS JIMMY'S gift to me for my fifty-sixth birthday, which he wrote in 2006 while attending Queen Mary University in London.].

Hi, Dad,

Happy belated birthday. I think I have finished this poem today for you, which brings me joy—a party favor! This poem I send to you, I will write again and again, as what it is about is the autonomy you have given me, which is the source of my confidence I have to write poems. A lot of men write because they are angry at their fathers, enmeshed by their fathers—I write instead to pursue freedom and distinction, potentials wholly given to me by you.

To count a good father a great provider
Concerns his heavy step with provisions.
Warmth in the loan of your yellow sweater,
And step by the sound of your slap-on-the-ass
Upon every taxi cab I ride in;
For I reckless tramp my hopeful, unsure path
With boldness pendent to your surety,
And the light in the throat, that leads
This burgeoning venture, must reckon
Still to the stops of the silent partner,
Who, with the power to scold, and mold,
Observes, and lets what he made self-fashion.
The gift of the myth of the Self-Made Man
Still seems the gift a Father gives,
A gift he firmly gives away.

Happy Birthday again, and thank you every time I chance to feel like I am doing what I want and need to do.

Love,

Jim

ACKNOWLEDGMENTS

THE STORIES ARE one hundred percent true, but we have used pseudonyms for some of the characters in respect of their privacy.

We are deeply grateful to so many who helped bring this book to final form. Emily Sue Buckberry, our dear friend. The girl from War strikes again! We are forever astonished and humbled by the stroke of fate that led you to our door and into our lives. We are blessed by your stewardship of my father's letter and your courage in reaching out after all those years—even though you had no idea what you were getting into! Steve Date. Blessings to the powers that made our paths through this universe intersect at that precise moment in the Coalwood vortex, for climbing into the rabbit hole with us and so beautifully telling our stories over these past six years. Steve says he is a better man because of it. I don't know a better man than Steve Date.

If Steve Date hadn't sent the stories of The Letter, Coalwood and Into The Light to Charlie Myers, who also has a strong Coalwood connection, and Charlie hadn't referred me to editor and writer Jan Weeks, this book would have taken much longer to shape. Weeks's deep, fearless spirituality, outstanding organizational skills, and expertise in finding the heart of the story have been invaluable in molding together my disparate tales. To my "Coach" and writer Marilyn Willison, for encouraging me very early on to write this story, repairing my butchered attempts at the first raw chapters and for living proof that there is nothing stronger than believing in yourself and the written word.

Our friends from Sedona, Tarra, Jade Wah'oo Grigori, and George Sanchez. Thank you for your extraordinary gifts and opening our minds, expanding our horizons and guiding us to the cracks where the light shines through. Deep gratitude to Dr. Frank Altobello for keeping his hands firmly on the rope as I went further into the rabbit hole and encouraging me to go ever deeper. To Keith Bennett and Pastor Jeremy Francis for making WriteMeSomethingBeautiful.com a reality, being early believers and invaluable assistance with helping us tell our story and share it with so many others. Danny Davis, my good friend and trainer, for keeping my body solid as my mind stretched to its limits, and for just being there with me every step as this story played out. My mother, the late Barbara Case Gauntt, for being such a pack rat and keeping all of the letters, photographs, report cards, newspaper clippings and journals, and most importantly your never-ending supply of strength, love, and glue in keeping our family together and tethered tightly to the pier as the storms raged around us. All blessings to my brother, Roshi Genro Gauntt, for being my snowplow in life, my teacher, and always being there for me when I've needed you the most. To my 'lil sister, Laura Gauntt Butie. I beg forgiveness for teasing and tormenting you so much as kids. You are the true Renaissance Woman, prematurely hardened with strength and yet always blessed with a pure beauty inside and out. Dad is proud of you and loves you so very much.

To our daughter, Brittany Kirby and son-in-law Ryan. Thank you for packing in with us as we've walked through this valley, for your immense love, compassion, and support, and for reminding us of the joy of new love, new life, and that forward is always a good direction.

To my fraternity brothers Richard Page, Greg Post, Jeff Schwartz, Mike Case, Denny Cline, Bill Canepa, Richard Dale, Ric Brown, Chip Conover, Bill Fawell, Jeff Miller, Gary Weiss, Hugh Sill, Philip Sanderson, Bill Driscoll, Buddy Wheaton, and George Blystone. To all of our fraternity brothers and sisters. This book is dedicated to our beloved sons and daughters who have crossed over before us. Suffering is hard work only made softer because we do it together.

To Hilary, My First Angel, my loving wife and best friend of over forty-four years. There would be nothing to write without you, for I would be nothing. You are everything to me. I will ride with you anywhere, any time, and for all time.

My father, Grover C. Gauntt, Jr. Thank you, Dad, for looking after your grandson, Jimmy, helping him over to the other side and reaching through to grab me as I was about to fall. You are the strongest man I know.

To James Tedrow Gauntt for showing us we never really lose the ones we love. I will be around, any time you want me, I'll be there—because I care more than you will ever know, my son. All love, Dad.

Made in the USA
Las Vegas, NV
01 April 2021